Creative Ideas for Qui

Sue Pickering is an Anglican priest and spiritual director.

She was born in the UK, but now lives in New Zealand, where she is a leader of retreats and Quiet Days.

Creative Ideas for Quiet Days

*Resources and liturgies
for retreats and
days of reflection*

Sue Pickering

CANTERBURY
PRESS
Norwich

First published in 2006 by the Canterbury Press Norwich
(a publishing imprint of Hymns Ancient & Modern Limited,
a registered charity)
13–17 Long Lane, London
EC1A 9PN

www.scm-canterburypress.co.uk

Second impression with CD

Reprinted 2010

Unless otherwise stated, Scripture quotations are taken from the
New Revised Standard Version, Division of Christian Education of
the National Council of the Churches of Christ in the United States
of America, 1989. Used by permission. All rights reserved.
'God of the Absurd' by Joy Cowley, *Aotearoa Psalms: Prayers of
a New People*, Pleroma Christian Supplies, New Zealand, 2004.
Used with permission of the publisher.
Two poems excerpted from *With Open Hands* by Henri J. M.
Nouwen. Copyright ©1972, 1995 by Ave Maria Press,
PO Box 428, Notre Dame, IN 46556, www.avemariapress.com.
Used with permission of the publisher.

British Library Cataloguing in Publication data

A catalogue record for this book is available
from the British Library

ISBN 978 1 85311 966 8

Typeset by Regent Typesetting, London
Printed and bound in UK by
MPG Books Ltd, Bodmin, Cornwall

This book is
for John who has loved me into life
for Matt who brings me great joy
for Marg who encouraged me,
with thanksgiving to God.

Contents

Foreword
By Margaret Silf

A comment I once heard during a day of reflection at a local retreat centre has never left me. It came from a woman who was juggling the needs of a growing family with the demands of full-time employment. 'This is the first time in fourteen years', she told us, 'that I have been away from family, home or work for as long as half a day.' I thought of those fourteen years, and reflected on the faithfulness of that woman's struggle to keep on nourishing her spiritual life, in the face of the unrelenting needs of other people, and the restless background noise of daily life in the fast lane.

Not everyone lives in the fast lane, of course. There are others who live alone, and crave for the companionship of fellow travellers on the spiritual path. How often have I heard the comment: 'I thought I was so alone. What a joy to share the journey, and to go deeper with God and with other pilgrims.'

All this convinces me that 'Quiet Days' answer a tremendous need in people, however overloaded, or lonely, their daily lives may be, and wherever they find themselves on the 'spiritual journey'. But how … ?

Sue Pickering provides us with a veritable feast of resource material for doing exactly that. If you have ever thought about offering a quiet day in your community or parish, but have taken fright at the thought of what it might entail, this book can take away your anxieties, and give you, in their place, a treasury of ideas and encouragement.

Sue has a special gift, not only in the inspiration she derives from her own life experience, but also her generosity in sharing it so freely. Through her gifts, we are invited to discover the living water in our own wells of everyday experience, to drink deeply, and to grow daily more closely attuned to the call of God in our hearts.

Introduction
Pools of provision from God

When I was nine, I went with my family, newly moved from the grey and smoky limitations of the post-war port of Liverpool, to the wild west-coast beach of Piha, just outside the sprawling city of Auckland, New Zealand.

I can still remember the joy and freedom of running barefoot over the dark heavy sand to get to the rock pools. I can still recollect the bliss of searching for treasures, and catching glimpses of life in another dimension, captivated by the smell of the sea coming fresh from the depths, its salty intensity undiluted by fog or fumes.

What mystery lay in those kelp-surging waters! What a delicious sense of manageable menace came to me then in the volatile form of red and purple crabs – bigger than anything I had ever encountered before – their skittering movement a sliding, chit-chat dance on the wet surface of the rocks as they sidled from my sight.

I was so enchanted by the whole event that I wanted to capture it, so I hid a dead red crab's shell in my pocket. When I got home, I wrapped it in cotton wool, safely (and tastefully) encased it in a flat red elastoplast tin rescued from the rubbish, and then conscientiously buried it in the lavendered depths of my woolly jumper drawer.

The winter was slow in cooling that year; my mind was soon taken by other pastimes and discoveries. The crabshell came to light only when a less than fragrant smell overcame my mother when she was sorting clothes several months later! I was scolded for my silliness and the crab, now drab, its riotous red ruined by decay, was thrown into the bin.

Now you may be wondering what on earth this story has to do with a book of resources for people running Quiet Days.

Quiet Days are in many ways like rock pools. They mirror the limited time available to us between 'the tides' of life's routines which govern our day; as 'Pools of provision' they offer a few hours in which to explore what might be revealed about God's goodness and sustaining love; they encourage contemplation and the chance to be caught up in the mystery of creation, to become children again, surprised by discoveries about ourselves and the God who invites us to intimacy.

Rock pools are attractive – there is always the possibility that something wonderful will be revealed in the next one that we investigate – and we know from our experience of God that there is indeed always something 'more' – for our God is a creative God who cannot help but engage in the creative process and longs to include us.

Rock pools require a certain discipline of stillness and attention. How easy it is to give a pool only a passing glance because there seems to be little of interest. But, when we make ourselves stop and wait and watch, we may find that a tiny movement takes our attention and we witness something special – a starfish tentacle smoothing a rocky hold, or a flash of tiny fish caught in the sunlight. So it can be as God's delicate touch – a wisp of the Spirit's breath, a tender Word, a minute shift in our interior landscape – tiptoes into the receptivity of our silence.

When the surface of the pool is disturbed by wind or made opaque by clouds' cover, we are reminded of life's demands and how hard it can be to make significant space to honour the interior life and give attention to our personal well-being. In rock pools we catch glimpses of shy creatures retreating into safety, like ideas whose life is not yet ready to be seen. With patience and time, both will reappear and allow their reality to be explored and appreciated.

Even though there may be other people around us or noisy activities nearby, we can still adopt an interior silence and 'contemplate' – look closely at our reality – whether that reality be the embryonic signs of life being nurtured near the vastness of the ocean, or other aspects of the creation: part of the woods nearby, the flight of a fantail, or the neighbour's baby learning to walk.

As we intentionally move away from the bustle of busyness into the rhythms of the natural world once again, we are reminding ourselves of our humanity and mortality, our blossoming and our beauty, our fragility and our fruitfulness.

Most important of all, we are giving our passionate, ever pursuing God the chance to catch up and sit awhile with us in the companionable silence only lovers share.

The intention of this book is to make available some of the resources which have been gathered over the past few years as I have conducted Quiet Days for parishes and ecumenical groups.

I hope that busy and experienced leaders may find ideas here, and that those engaging in this ministry for the first time may find themselves reassured and encouraged enough to step out; whoever chooses to use this material is invited to make it their own in whatever way maintains its integrity. Individuals who want to give shape to a time of personal reflection may also find help and hints here.

The purchase of this book entitles you to photocopy or print out those pages marked with a 🐚 in Part Two, Themed Resources for Quiet Days, for personal or non-profit use as required, e.g. for distribution to participants in Quiet Days, days of reflection or similar contemplative opportunities.

Part One
Getting started

What is a Quiet Day?

'Quiet Day' is a term commonly used for a day set apart to listen to God. Other ways of describing such a time include 'Retreat Day' or 'Day of Reflection'.

Why bother setting time apart?

So many people today comment on the pace of life and the difficulty of finding enough time to fit in all the tasks which seem to be demanded by our modern twenty-first-century Western lifestyle. There are complaints of time going too fast, of not enough hours in the day, of the never-ending demands of others; people are getting 'burnt out' as they try to juggle multiple roles, meet work obligations or minister to others.

Jesus knew only too well what it was like to be at everyone's beck and call. Once word got out about the signs and wonders he was performing, he was followed by people who were just as hungry and determined as modern paparazzi. No matter where he went, he was recognized and was expected to meet the needs of those who were present.

But there was one way that Jesus could find the peace he needed: he would go out, either at night or very early in the morning, when there were few people around, to have time for prayer and renewal. He did this particularly in times of stress, such as after the beheading of John the Baptist; in times of decision-making, for example when choosing his disciples (Luke 6.12–13); and in times of exhaustion when he needed renewal from God, the Source of all power and healing, for example after the feeding of the five thousand (Mark 6.30–46).

If Jesus, the Son of God, the closest person to God's heart, needed to seek solitude and deep connection with God, how much more do we need to spend time apart in God's healing presence, so we can be refreshed and enabled for what lies ahead in our day. How can we, dare we, think that we can manage life's considerable demands without the sort of focused contemplative time with the Creator and Sustainer of all things, which Jesus knew he needed and made sure he took.

Some people believe that they must always put other people's needs ahead of their own, even to the point of exhaustion. Yet we are encouraged to respect our physical body as the temple of the living God (1 Cor. 6.19–20) and are reminded of the need for regular rest for body, mind and spirit in the commandment 'Remember the Sabbath day . . .' (Exodus 31.14 – 17).

But there is another reason for setting time apart. If we commit ourselves to spending time listening to God, we are more likely to 'hear' God's 'word' to us, however that 'word' may be conveyed, whether through Scripture, a song lyric, a comment from a friend, even a 'chance' piece of overheard conversation. But we do not deepen our relationship with God solely for our own benefit. Modern writers such as Gerard

3

Hughes[1] and Kenneth Leech[2] abhor the rise of 'privatized spirituality', an extension of the Western preoccupation with individualism and individualization into the realm of the spirit. Instead we must be very clear that the blessings we receive through our developing intimacy with God are there to be shared.

We are being strengthened and healed for a purpose: so that we can, in our turn, be bearers of God's grace to those we meet; so we can be agents of God's justice in the systems of which we are a part, whether the microsystems of our families, church or school, or the less comfortable macrosystems of local, national or even global politics.

Discerning the expression of our ministry takes time, energy, trust and a commitment. Attending a Quiet Day is one way of ensuring that we make space in our busy schedule. It is like putting an 'AT HOME' sign at the window of our soul, so God can see we are ready to listen. Although God may indeed call us into something which challenges us to the very core of our being, we can be reassured that we will be equipped and empowered whenever we say 'Yes!' to God's invitation.

Freedom and Structure

The degree of structure required for a Quiet Day reflects the nature and experience of those taking part. For example, if people are coming to a Quiet Day as a first step in exploring silence and contemplation, most will be helped by having an idea of what to expect during the course of the day. They may need to have some organized activities to help give shape to the day; they may appreciate having a theme to use as a point of reference for their thoughts and prayer.

If, on the other hand, the participants have been coming to Quiet Days for many years, they may need less 'input' from a facilitator. Previous experience gives them the confidence to let the day unfold as they relax, trusting God's willingness to meet them as and when the time is right.

In either case, we know that, in offering a Quiet Day, as leaders all we are doing is providing a context in which people can be encouraged to listen for 'that still, small voice' as God woos them like a lover. All the 'formal' elements of the day – the suggested structure, the short 'talks', the reflection material, the opening and closing worship, the music, the setting – are there solely to support participants as they listen and wait for the touch of God.

For that reason, no matter what the level of experience individuals have, I am very clear in encouraging them to take or leave the various aspects of the day, so they can be free to attend to whatever God is doing in this set-apart time, without feeling that they have to stop and conform to a schedule.

---

1 Gerard W. Hughes, *God of Surprises*, Darton, Longman and Todd, London, 1985.

2 Kenneth Leech, *Soul Friend: Spiritual Direction in the Modern World* (revised edition), Morehouse, Pennsylvania, 2001, pp. xiii–xix.

Below, you will find an outline of two Quiet Day structures which will give you some idea of how you might like to arrange a day yourself. Even though your situation may require a different format, I always think it is helpful to have a starting-point when you are trying to plan!

A more detailed sample programme sheet is included in the Appendix. This sheet gives the date, venue, times and theme of the Quiet Day, and offers some ideas on how to enter into the silence. If you would like a copy of this sheet emailed to you so you can amend it for your own use, please contact me on suepickering@xtra.co.nz.

Sample programme 1[3]

9.30   Gather for registration. Tea, coffee available all day.

9.45   A brief introduction to the concept of the Quiet Day and to Silence.

10.00   Opening worship followed by a short talk on the theme.

10.30   Silence begins (reflection sheets provided).

12.00   Prayer at midday (optional).

12.15   Participants have lunch when they are ready. Silence is maintained but quiet music is played in the background.

12.45   A second short talk may be followed by a guided meditation on Scripture and further time for silent reflection.

2.15   Gathering in the lounge.

2.30   Closing Eucharist, *agape* meal and/or sharing of symbols.

3.00   Home-going.

Sample programme 2

9.00   Gather for registration. Tea, coffee available all day . . .

9.15   Opening worship followed by a short talk on the theme.

9.45   Silence begins. Lunch is taken when each person is ready.

12.45   A time of sharing in pairs/small groups followed by a second short talk or a guided meditation.

1.30   Further time for silent reflection.

3.30   Gathering in the lounge for the closing liturgy/ritual.

4.00   Home-going.

You will notice that the second example is slightly longer, less structured and differs significantly from the first sample by including time for sharing in pairs or small groups.

The various elements (leader's input, silent reflection, worship, sharing, music, formal prayer, closing liturgy, etc.) can be used in any combination according to the needs of the group and your own situation.

---

3 Based on a National Retreat Association brochure (UK).

Depending on your own background, you may or may not be in a position to offer half-hour slots of time for individuals to talk to you about their faith journey during the times of reflection. If you are a spiritual director or have experience in companioning others, it can be helpful to provide a list of times when you are available, for people to fill in as they sign in for the Quiet Day. Placing a tick by a time slot secures that time for the individual and protects his or her privacy.

Similarly, you may or may not prefer to close with a Communion according to the liturgy of your tradition and the presence/absence of a priest, pastor or licensed minister. An *agape* meal or other reverent sharing of bread and wine accompanied by the reading of the Scriptures may be a helpful substitute, especially when people from a number of denominations are present.

Sometimes it can be a beautiful gift to encourage participants to share something of what they have received from God during the day – their own 'gospel'. However, this invitation must always leave an opportunity for people to 'pass' or to offer a symbol without speaking, so that individuals are not placed in an awkward situation if they are currently in 'the desert' in terms of experiencing God or are still savouring a moment of grace.

Silence

Silence is a rarity for many of us in today's society. We are constantly bombarded with external noise from the moment we are shocked into wakefulness by our alarm clocks, to the moment we wearily switch off the television before we go to bed at night. Computers, telephones, machinery, planes flying overhead, traffic, voices . . . How hard it is to quell the clamour of the outside world in order to hear the stillness at our centre.

Yet not everyone welcomes the silence and time for personal reflection which a Quiet Day provides.

Some people are put off a Quiet Day because they are uncertain about how they will manage the silence. If they are of an extrovert temperament and used to engaging others in conversation, it is especially difficult to contemplate a few hours without such connection. Realizing that there are scheduled times when speaking is part of the programme can be a relief! Providing some suggestions about how to engage with the silence can also be helpful.

Others may resist silence because of unhappy childhood associations. Silence, in some households, might have been used as a sign of the withdrawal of parental affection, or have been imposed as a punishment – a consequence of being banished to one's room or even, tragically, locked in a cupboard and left in the dark.

Even though people have come along to a Quiet Day because they want to grow closer to God, they may need support as they encounter the silent sections of the day. A short talk about the nature of the day, together with ways of being with the silence, can be helpful. Providing a chance for participants to share something of their experience of silence at the beginning of the day can free them to enter the experience more hopefully. Five or ten minutes in pairs is all that is needed, with each person responding to the question 'What has my experience of silence been?'

After the Opening Worship and first Short Talk, offering the silence to each other as a gift, like sharing the peace, can help to overcome some people's anxiety. Reassuring participants that you are there for them to speak to, if they need to discuss something, can also provide a helpful 'backstop'.

INTERIOR SILENCE

The quieting of the imagination,
feelings and rational faculties
in the process of recollection;
the general loving attentiveness
to God in pure faith.
Thomas Keating[4]

Practicalities

Quiet days may be held anywhere: a small under-used rural church, a hall in a large city parish complex, a purpose-built retreat centre, a special outdoor setting by a lake or in a garden, or in the living room of a generous friend.[5]

For the day to flow smoothly it can help to consider a number of factors as you make your choice:

Accessibility	in case a participant has mobility problems or a certain level of fitness is required, especially in outdoor venues
Distance	generally transport can be shared if people need to travel; going on a journey to get to the venue can enhance the sense of expectation and add to the experience
Noise	is the venue going to be reasonably quiet or under the local airport flight path?! Are there cell phones which need turning off?
Interruptions	can you guarantee that you will be free from interruption by other users of the venue so that participants are free to concentrate on their time with God?

---

4 Thomas Keating, *Open Heart: The Contemplative Dimension of the Gospel*, Continuum, London, 2002, p. 146.

5 One word of caution about using a friend's home: it is often very hard for that person to participate fully in the Quiet Day as she/he is likely to be distracted by the group's practical needs and the effort involved in getting things ready for the day.

Temperature	when people are sitting still or moving slowly, a drop in temperature of the venue can affect their concentration. You may need to encourage people to bring a rug or to wear warm clothing.
Comfort	toilet facilities and comfortable seating are also factors to be considered; some people may need to bring their own chair, so they can minimize their discomfort and pay attention to God
Kitchen facilities	most people appreciate being able to get a hot drink during the course of a Quiet Day – you may need to ask participants to bring a thermos!
Cost	most church or private home facilities can be made available at little or no cost; it is important that both facilitator and host are reimbursed for their expenses and, if appropriate, the facilitator is offered something for his/her time in preparing and conducting the Quiet Day. However, this must be balanced against the absolute necessity of making this opportunity available to as wide a range of people as possible. Using a donation system with a suggested level of contribution, can be a fair method of handling financial considerations.

Music

We all have music which has powerfully connected us to the divine – it might be a mighty operatic aria, a poignant violin passage, a complex concerto or a modern pop song whose lyrics touch our hearts.

It would be impossible to list all the musical resources which might suit a particular group, but below I have listed a range of CDs which are readily available and which cover a range of styles and preferences:

'Songs of Taizé' Boxed Set Double CD, Kingsway Music KMCD2210
(contemplative songs, simple repeated chants, retails for around £16.99, available through most Christian bookstores)

'Songs from a Secret Garden', Secret Garden Polygram 1996 528 230-2
'Once in a red moon', Secret Garden Universal 2002 548 678-2
(contemporary violin and piano, instrumental and vocal reflective music)

'The most relaxing classical album in the world . . . ever!'
36 track double CD EMI 7243 5 66650 2 6
(one example of a low-cost classical compilation – others are available)

Checklist of items to take to your Quiet Day

As a Girl Guide, I was taught to BE PREPARED and I have learned from experience that *all* of the items listed below may be needed at some point in a Quiet Day:

- Enough photocopied sheets for participants to have their own copy of the programme for the day, opening worship sheet and the reflections.
- Bible and Concordance.
- Copies of resources for midday prayer and/or communion.
- Props associated with the theme.
- Candles, matches, cloth, resources and focal item, such as cross, flowers, photo, icon suitable for opening worship.
- A box for the donation (and perhaps a few pound coins or £5 notes for change if you have time to arrange that).
- A list of names, addresses and contact details for those who attend to complete, so you can advise them of further contemplative events in your area.
- A CD player and extension cord.
- Music suitable for the theme.
- Crayons or felt-tip pens, scissors and glue-stick.
- Spare paper for writing or drawing.
- Playdough – see recipe at back of book.
- Tea, coffee, milk, sugar (and biscuits if you need them!).
- Tissues.
- If your tradition includes the sacrament of anointing, then it can be very helpful to have anointing oil available.
- Bread and wine, chalice and paten, purificator and cloth for table, and any other items you want to use for a worship focus and communion at the end of the Quiet Day.
- A few slim books related to prayer, contemplation, the Christian journey, and so on, may be included if you have access to them. Some people need a little extra reading – others are content to use the Scripture and reflection sheets only. Do keep a list of the books you bring so that you can keep track of them!
- Your own mobile phone, especially in remoter areas, just in case!

Using the imagination; engaging the emotions

Praying with Scripture using the imagination is not a new idea or one that we need shy away from. Generally this prayer takes one of two possible forms:

- projecting ourselves back into a Bible passage using all our senses to assist our imagination of that scene or event (often called Ignatian prayer)
- applying the words of Scripture to our current situation by imagining how we might react or what Jesus might say about the issues we are facing (Augustinian prayer)[6]

However, before they begin to use this method, some Christians need to face their deep suspicion of the imagination, a suspicion which comes from a fear that this faculty could provide easy entry for the deceitful work of the enemy.

John Powell describes the dilemma faced by many:

Somehow the same people who believe that God can enter the mind with his ideas and perspectives, the will with his strength and desires, or the emotions with his peace, balk at the thought that God can stimulate the imagination to hear inwardly actual words or see actual visions . . .[7]

Richard Foster speaks of 'sanctifying the imagination', acknowledging the fears of those who think it could be misused:

. . . the imagination, like all our faculties, has participated in the fall. But just as we believe that God can take our reason (fallen as it is) and sanctify it and use it for his good purposes, so we believe he can sanctify the imagination and use it for his good purposes . . . God created us with an imagination, and, as Lord of his creation, he can and does redeem it and use it for the work of the kingdom of God.[8]

Why should we consider the imagination when we have the opportunity to study the Scriptures using our reason? What is there about the use of the imagination that makes it such a valuable tool for helping us to encounter Jesus and for helping us to heal? Different writers offer a range of reasons.

Joyce Huggett describes the imagination as 'the key that unlocks the inner world of our personality: the "heart"'.[9] She goes on to say that, as prayer is the language of

---

6 See Chester E. Michael and Marie C. Norrisey, *Prayer and Temperament: Different Prayer Forms for Different Personality Types*, The Open Door, Virginia, 1991.

7 John Powell, *He Touched Me*, Argus, Niles, Illinois, 1974, pp. 78–9.

8 Richard Foster, *Prayer: Finding the Heart's True Home*, Hodder & Stoughton, London, 1992, p. 15.

9 Joyce Huggett, *Open to God*, Hodder & Stoughton, London, 1989, p. 54.

a love relationship between the individual praying and God, picture language helps us to explore and experience that relationship in a way that concepts, understood through the intellect, cannot.

Richard Foster writes:

> To believe that God can sanctify and utilise the imagination is simply to take seriously the Christian idea of incarnation. God so accommodates, so enfleshes himself into our world, that he uses the images we know and understand to teach us about the unseen world of which we know so little, and find so difficult to understand.[10]

Sheila Pritchard, in her recent book, *The Lost Art of Meditation*, comments:

> Jesus called on people's imagination all the time. He was constantly telling stories and painting word pictures. He asked people to imagine the kingdom of God as a mustard seed, as yeast, as treasure hidden in a field . . . every time we take the bread and wine at a communion service, we use our imagination to enter the reality of Jesus' body broken and blood poured out for us.[11]

Alexander Whyte writes of the invitation we are given to enter the Scriptures:

> You open your New Testament . . . and by your imagination, that moment you are one of Christ's disciples on the spot, and are at his feet . . . with your imagination anointed with holy oil . . . at one time, you are the publican: at another time the prodigal . . . at another time, you are Mary Magdalene: at another time, you are Peter in the porch.[12]

In considering the link between emotions and the imagination, Marlene Halpin says:

> Imagination and emotions are related . . . They are designed to contribute to our awareness of experience: both pleasing and displeasing, pleasurable and painful, satisfying or harmful. Not only do they provide consciousness of the moment's interactions, they contribute to our decision making . . . [S]table people are aware of what is happening, how they are responding. They are not unfeeling or unresponsive, but, because of their emotional truthfulness, they are able to live fully and interact wisely with their environment and the people around them.[13]

---

10 Foster, *Prayer*, p. 15.

11 Sheila Pritchard, *The Lost Art of Meditation: Deepening Your Prayer Life*, Scripture Union, Bletchley, 2003, p. 43.

12 Alexander Whyte, *Lord, Teach Us To Pray*, Harper & Brothers, New York (no date), p. 251.

13 Marlene Halpin, *Imagine That! Using Phantasy in Spiritual Direction*, Wm C. Brown, Iowa, 1982, pp. 27–8.

The imagination then helps us connect on a heart level with God, it helps us to deepen our participation in the divine mystery of the incarnation and it gives us an opportunity to be part of the scriptures by entering into the event as fully as we can, making ourselves open to an encounter with the Living Christ.

Guided meditation: a way of using our imagination

As facilitators, we need to be aware of our own levels of competence before we consider including a guided meditation in a Quiet Day. Marlene Halpin, comments on the need to be responsible in our use of guided imagination.[14]

For me this means that the facilitator:

- has had some experience of participating in guided meditation or fantasy work before offering a guided meditation to others
- has someone (for example a supervisor or mentor) with whom to discuss the wisdom of including this element in the Quiet Day. It is wise for example to ensure that no-one in the group is suffering from a serious mental illness
- makes it explicit to participants that there is no obligation to take part in the guided imagination exercise AND that they are free to 'opt out' at any stage of the exercise if they wish
- provides a context in which the guided meditation fits naturally, so that it emerges from earlier discussion or input and is followed by a chance to process whatever has occurred, either with another person, or through journalling, or in a time of reflection
- has sufficient trust in the Holy Spirit, that he/she can offer this activity without having any control or knowledge about how each person will respond.

The guided meditations in this collection of resources are designed to be open-ended: the leader will guide the meditation only to the point where there is an invitation to connect with God or Jesus. Beyond this point, participants are free to let the meditation unfold in a way that is personally appropriate.

Once people have had time to be with their experience, say after around five minutes, the leader makes some appropriate comments to bring the activity to a conclusion and enable engagement with the rest of the day.

A suggested text for each guided meditation is provided. When a pause is indicated, this is marked with a series of dots . . . Further comments for leaders are inserted in (*brackets*).

Most people benefit from being able to process their guided meditation experience a little further. Provisions for this can include inviting people to share something with one other person, encouraging people to make notes or drawings in their journal, or making yourself available to listen to an experience or explore a question.

---

14 Ibid., pp. 32–3.

Again it is important to make this optional so people are free to keep working with what has emerged without distraction or intrusion. Sometimes a touch of grace is better not shared until the person has taken it more deeply into their experience and belief.

Note: Not everyone finds this way of praying comes naturally. For some, pictures don't seem to form in the mind; instead there is an 'intellectual vision', an 'inner knowing', an awareness that defies description rather than a definite sense of a place or person. This means that in any group of people at a Quiet Day, there will be some for whom this method may not be immediately fruitful. Encourage people not to struggle with the guided meditation exercises, but simply to participate if they want to and let God do the rest. If you have any doubt about using a guided meditation then it is wise to set this aspect of the Quiet Day aside.

Personal preparation and process

So 'your bags are packed and you're ready to go'[15] – or are you?

No matter how much experience we have in facilitating events like a Quiet Day, or standing up in front of others, speaking and taking responsibility for the content and smooth running of the programme, there will be times when we have doubts about our readiness or ability to work with a particular group at a particular time.

Those of us who are leading Quiet Days recognize the benefit of spending time in prayer before undertaking this ministry. If we are fortunate, we have prayerful people who will support the day and its preparation. We can do our best to spend time the week or day before the event, holding before God those who will attend, praying for the grace and wisdom we need as we facilitate the day. If we do not take this time apart, we are in danger of finding ourselves caught up in the whirlpool of busyness and we are left with the painful irony of facilitating for others the very thing we need for ourselves.

If, however, circumstances conspire against our reflective preparation, we can still have confidence in God's provision. If we are turned towards God as a telescope is turned towards the vastness of space, we can be assured that God's invisible waves of grace will ripple towards us and those who set aside time to 'tune in'.

If we sense God's call to offer this type of day in our parish or community, even if we wonder about our ability or our experience, nevertheless with prayer and preparation we can use these and other resources to do 'something beautiful for God'.[16]

God honours those who take the time to listen to the still, small voice of the Holy One and we are blessed simply by being witnesses to the movement of grace in the hearts and lives of those we accompany.

> A toe in the water?
>> May the streams of the Spirit refresh you
> Up to your ankles?
>> May the currents of God caress you
> Over your knees?
>> May waves of Christ-confidence surround you
> Out of your depth?
>> May oceans of Grace uphold and embrace you.

> AMEN
>> and AMEN
>>> and AMEN.

---

15 Adapted from a song by The Seekers, 'Leavin' on a jet plane'.
16 Malcolm Muggeridge, *Something Beautiful for God*, Collins, London, 1971.

Part Two
Themed resources for Quiet Days

Themed resources for Quiet Days

In the pages which follow, material is provided for twelve Quiet Days, each on a different theme. The Quiet Days included are suitable for people at various stages of their faith journey, and are designed not only to help people deepen their relationship with God but also to discover more about themselves.

All have an opening worship section, using a simple candle-lighting ritual which three of the participants can do. Depending on the time available for additional preparation and the needs of your group, you can adapt this as you see fit, for example by adding music, and/or inviting several participants to add symbols to a worship focus or small altar to help illustrate the theme.

All have suggested morning and afternoon input in the form of short talks or discussions (about 3–5 minutes each), as well as a range of material on the theme, including Scripture references, questions for reflection, and poetry.[17] In some cases, there are suggestions which would suit people who prefer visual responses, who like to use colour and drawing to express their journey with God or who would prefer some active options during the day. Guidelines for facilitators are included in bracketed italics.

Some Quiet Days would be more appropriate at a particular part of the church year or season. 'The foolishness of God' and 'Rolling back the stone' lend themselves to a spring or Easter reflection, while 'The waiting place of God' might be best used in autumn or Advent. The table on the next page gives an indication of when a particular Quiet Day may be most suitable, whether in terms of the time of the year or the needs of the group.

'Stepping out of the boat' is a little different from the other Quiet Days. It is designed primarily as a group process and is suitable for parish council/vestry or other groups who want to dream of new expressions of church, or together face issues of change or challenge. This Quiet Day deliberately encourages the facilitator to explore some useful websites with particular relevance to this theme.

In Part Three of the book you will find some additional prayers and blessings to include in your closing worship if you wish.

ENJOY!

---

17 Unless otherwise acknowledged, all poetry is by Sue Pickering and is hitherto unpublished.

Finding your way around the resources

Quiet Day	Page	Opening worship	Talks + resources sheets	Suitable for theme or occasion	Guided meditation
Homecoming	19	✓	✓ + 3	encouragement; God's love for each person	✓
Retreat and advance	28	✓	✓ + 2	invitation to silence in God; church or small group time away	-
Crampons and crevasses	35	✓	✓ + 3	risk, dependency on God	-
Rolling back the stone	43	✓	✓ + 3	Easter – our own faith journey; helping others grow in God	✓
The foolishness of God	52	✓	✓ + 4	Easter – the cross; entrusting us with the Good News	-
Transition	61	✓	✓ + 2	seeing times of change as potential gifts of grace	-
What's in a name?	67	✓	✓ + 2	how we see God; how God might see us	✓
Greed and grace	76	✓	✓ + 3	holding on and letting go – opening to God's grace	-
Choose life!	85	✓	✓ + 4	recognizing God's persistent call; abundant life	✓
Stepping out of the boat	94	✓	✓ + 2	parish reflection on the future and mission; moving out in faith	-
The waiting place of God	101	✓	✓ + 2	Advent – Mary and the place of waiting in her life and ours	✓
Mosaics of mercy	108	✓	✓ + 4	integrating our experiences; 'examen' (reflection at day's end); our place in our community	-

Homecoming
Opening worship

SENTENCE OF THE DAY

If a shepherd has a hundred sheep, and one of them has gone astray, does he not leave the ninety-nine on the mountains and go in search of the one that went astray? And if he finds it, truly I tell you, he rejoices over it more than over the ninety-nine that never went astray.
Matthew 18.12–13

Leader   God of journey, we thank you for bringing us here today, for gathering us together at this point in our own individual lives, so that we may spend time with you in corporate solitude.

All   **Gracious God, we come from the busyness of our daily lives into your peace. Help us to leave our responsibilities and preoccupations behind for a few hours.**
May we come to know you more clearly this day.

FIRST CANDLE IS LIT

Leader   We thank you, God of Love, that you are more than ready to receive us, that you welcome us whether we come from a distance or from close by, whether we come to you doubtful or hurt or worried or angry or guilty.

All   **Loving God, some of us carry heavy baggage from the past that has held us back in our search for you. Help us to leave our fears and failures behind us.**

SECOND CANDLE IS LIT

Leader   We thank you that you offer us a permanent home within your Love, a home within which we can feel safe, accepted, free to grow into the people you created us to be.

All   **Homemaker God, help us to explore the home you have prepared within us where your Spirit dwells.**
May we come to enjoy that home together today and in the days to come. Amen.

THIRD CANDLE IS LIT

Homecoming – short talk 1

This Quiet Day has for its theme 'Homecoming . . . Coming Home to God' but perhaps we might begin by looking at homecoming in human terms.

There are all sorts of homecomings:

- There are unexpected homecomings after years away; people come home carrying a series of successes and adventures to relate or maybe carrying disappointment, guilt or even shame; during their absence, there have been lots of changes, changes in those left behind and in the one returning; perhaps there are feelings of uncertainty and anxiety about the welcome mixed in with the anticipation of the homecoming.
- There are homecomings in which people have been away for a few months, perhaps visiting once or twice a year; there might be a few changes in between visits but generally there is no real anxiety about the return and it doesn't take too long before it feels 'like home'.
- And then there is the homecoming after a five-minute trip to the shop to get some milk or bread; such a familiar homecoming that it is rarely given a moment's notice . . . we all take it for granted day after day and overlook the wonder of it.

And so it is as we come home to God.

We all know people who feel as if they have been away from God for quite some time; perhaps they hardly know the way home any more . . . but we know the Holy Spirit is at work to encourage them back towards an awareness of God in their lives . . . and maybe you will have a part to play in their return.

We know others who could be called occasional visitors, only calling on God when things get tough, praying only in emergencies, getting together with other Christians at Easter or Christmas, perhaps thinking about reading their Bible but somehow never quite getting round to it.

We may be in daily contact with God and have a regular practice of prayer and Bible study, sharing with other Christians on a regular basis; we may feel as if we are never far from home . . . but there is still a sense that there is something more . . . for God is always calling us closer, wanting us to enjoy all that His home has to offer: healing and love and freedom and joy.

In the introduction to his book, *Prayer: Finding the Heart's True Home*,[18] Richard Foster writes:

Coming home: an invitation to prayer

God has graciously allowed me to catch a glimpse into his heart, and I want to share with you what I have seen. Today the heart of God is an open wound of love. He aches over our distance and our preoccupation. He mourns that we do not draw near to him. He grieves that we have forgotten him.

He weeps over our obsession with muchness and manyness. He longs for our presence. And he is inviting you – and me – to come home, to come home to where we belong, to come home to that for which we were created.

His arms are stretched out wide to receive us. His heart is enlarged to take us in. For too long we have been in a far country: a country of noise and hurry and crowds, a country of climb and push and shove, a country of frustration and fear and intimidation. And he welcomes us home: home to serenity and peace and joy, home to friendship and fellowship and openness, home to intimacy and acceptance and affirmation.

We do not need to be shy. He invites us into the living-room of his heart where we can put on slippers and share freely. He invites us into the kitchen of his friendship where chatter and batter mix in good fun. He invites us into the dining-room of his strength where we can feast to our heart's delight. He invites us into the study of his wisdom where we can learn, and grow and stretch . . . and ask all the questions we want.

He invites us into the workshop of his creativity, where we can be co-labourers with him, working together to determine the outcome of events. He invites us into the bedroom of his rest where new peace is found and we can be naked and vulnerable and free. It is also the place of deepest intimacy where we are known to the fullest.

The key to this home, this heart of God is prayer.

---

18 Richard Foster, *Prayer: Finding the Heart's True Home*, Hodder & Stoughton, London, 1992, pp. 1–2.

Homecoming – reflection sheet 1

Consider what it would be like to journey home to God.
What feelings or thoughts are uppermost?
What do you need to help you as you move nearer to the One
who longs for your return?

HOMECOMING

Do you hesitate, distance-safe, out of reach,
or so you think, of Love?

Do you crawl, exhausted and life-battered,
guilty and uncertain?

Do you walk, dragging memory-heavy thoughts
as laden bags behind you?

Or do you run, eyes purposeful, fixed on your dream destination,
ready to be enveloped
in the waiting arms of God?

Promises from Scripture to give you confidence as you journey home to God:

Jesus said: 'Come to me all you that are weary and are carrying heavy burdens, and I will give you rest.' *Matthew 11.28*	Then I saw a new heaven and a new earth . . . 'See, the home of God is among mortals. He will dwell with them, and they will be his peoples, and God himself will be with them, and be their God.' *Revelation 21.1–3*	A new heart I will give you, and a new spirit I will put within you; I will remove from your body the heart of stone and give you a heart of flesh. *Ezekiel 36.26*

Homecoming – short talk 2

This morning we have been spending time in quietness reflecting on how much God desires for us to come home to Him and how important prayer is as the key to entering the heart of God.

Perhaps we have discovered that there are some things about ourselves that make coming home to God hard for us. Perhaps there are aspects of our personality or lifestyle that make prayer difficult for us even though we want to pray.

Perhaps there may be upsetting circumstances at home or family worries which threaten to overwhelm us, even though we long to have the strength to rise above them. We may be troubled by habits that seem to control us – we may long for the fruits of the Spirit to be manifest in our life but still find ourselves being anything but joyful and loving or self-controlled.

Be reassured that the simple fact of desiring to grow in God is a sign of God's grace at work in you!

How can we move closer to the God who calls us?

In our Christian journey, we are encouraged to love God with all our heart, mind, soul and strength and to love our neighbours as we love ourselves. We are rightly aware of the call to love God; we spend a lot of energy on loving our neighbours – perhaps through acts of service and support. But for many of us, the phrase 'love ourselves' has dropped into disuse and we rarely take the time to 'be our own best friend'.

Some of the reasons for this lie in our readiness to confuse selfishness with self-care. We strive to avoid selfishness, and rightly so, because there is a tempting attraction to self-centredness in all of us. But – a bit like throwing out the baby with the bathwater – in trying to avoid selfishness, we may neglect our legitimate needs.

If we think of Jesus and how he coped with the enormous demands made on him, we see him taking time at regular intervals to spend time alone, time to pray and to be with God. We also see him going to the home of friends to rest and be renewed among people who loved him. Was that selfishness on his part?

Of course not, because we can see how necessary it was for him.

How much more necessary is it for us to spend time in caring for ourselves, in giving our bodies rest, our minds peace and our spirits space and nourishment.

How important it is for us to take the time to get to know ourselves really well: weaknesses and strengths, addictions and freedoms.

We do this not to reinforce self-centredness but because, as Thomas à Kempis wrote: 'A humble knowledge of thyself is a surer way to God than a deep search after learning.'[19]

---

19 Thomas à Kempis, *The Imitation of Christ*.

As we get to know ourselves better, stop pretending, take off the masks we wear out in the world; as we face who we really are, we are then able to bring who we really are to God for healing and forgiveness and redemption.

And when we do this, we experience the wonder of knowing ourselves to be loved by God, *being accepted as we are*. This in turn helps us to be more accepting of others. We withdraw our projections and, instead of being preoccupied with blaming others for the difficulties in our lives, we spend time co-operating with God as the work of redemption takes shape in us.

Homecoming – a guided meditation

In a guided meditation, it is your choice whether you take part or not. You may prefer simply to listen without thinking about images or trying to make something significant surface. Just trust the Holy Spirit to begin what is right for you at this time – even if you do not become aware of any outcome at once.

Make sure that you are comfortable – take a few moments to relax yourself physically. . . . You are invited to close your eyes to minimize distractions. Once I have stopped speaking, either stay with what might have arisen for you or let it go gently. When you are ready you may like to write about or draw something of your experience, or you may prefer to continue with what emerged for you earlier in the day, or simply spend time resting in God until we gather for our Eucharist/closing.

So let us begin with a prayer:

Loving God, we bring to you this time of reflection using our imaginations.
May your Holy Spirit guide us and protect us, and reveal more of your nature which is Love. Amen.

Take a few easy, slow breaths . . . and begin to let yourself settle into the gentle warmth of God.

Now, very gently allow the picture of a home to come into focus for you.
It might be a place you know or somewhere that you have never seen before but which has the feel of home about it.

Just take a minute or two to let that take shape – remembering not to get anxious about trying to make it happen.

Now imagine yourself entering that home and finding your way to a room in which you feel really comfortable. Again, it might be a room you recognize or a room you have never actually seen before. But it's a room you are comfortable in . . . you feel welcomed and there is something about the room that enfolds you in peacefulness. Spend some time looking at the room in detail: notice what is on the floor . . . the walls . . . Look at the windows . . . the furniture . . . any ornaments or decorations . . .

(Allow a few moments for this image to settle and be explored a little.)

When you've finished exploring the room, you notice that over in one corner, lit by a shaft of sunlight, is a box you haven't noticed before.

You go over to it . . . You open the lid and inside you find something that God wants you to know about or to have a look at . . .

(Again allow a few moments for this part of the meditation to take shape.)

Examine what is inside the box – it may be something *visible*, in which case you can pick it up and look at it carefully, asking God about it if you are a bit uncertain; or it may be *invisible*, for example a quality like courage or hopefulness. If so, let yourself receive that quality as a gift, taking it deeper into yourself.

When you are ready, replace the item in the box and close the lid, or take it with you if that seems the appropriate thing to do.

(A few moments are needed here before . . .)

Retrace your steps through the home and out of the front door into the garden. Gradually allow yourself to come back to this place and this time, remembering that you can return to this place of welcome in your imagination if you wish.

(Depending on the group, you may like to invite them to write about this experience in their journals or provide some time for them to talk about it in pairs.)

Homecoming – reflection sheet 2

You may like to consider drawing your way home to God – perhaps putting colour on this outline, or making a path with some of the helps and hindrances to your homecoming placed on or around it.

Take time to invite the Holy Spirit into this process, especially if you encounter any obstacles to finding your way home to God.

Once you have finished, talk to Jesus about what you have discovered.

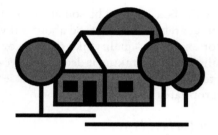

Homecoming – additional resource

COME HOME TO THE HEARTH OF MY HEART

'My dear one,' God says,
'I want you to see into my Being.'

'The cells in my heart
hold people you pray for,
each one kept safe
in my love and provision.

There are cells beyond number,
some sparkling, some shining,
some throbbing with pain,
but enough to embrace
the whole of creation:
all people,
all faiths,
all creatures,
all trees and all mountains,
all stars and all depths,
all questions, all struggles,
all barely grasped answers,
all efforts to better
the lot of the poor ones,
all deaths and disasters,
and all resurrections,
no matter how small they may seem.

Come home to the hearth of my heart;
to the warmth that awaits you
in the solace of silence.
Rest from your journey
and relax in my love.'

So I did,
and I do,
and I will.

Retreat and advance
Opening worship

SENTENCE OF THE DAY
They that wait upon the Lord shall renew their strength; they shall mount up with wings as eagles; they shall run, and not be weary; and they shall walk, and not faint.
Isaiah 40.31, AV

Leader We thank you Lord for bringing us here today, for gathering us together at this point in our own journeys so that we may spend time with you in companionable solitude.
May we know again the reality of your provision for each of us, according to our needs and your call in our lives.

All **We are surrounded by audible noise and the bustle of daily living. TV and telephone, machinery and mowers, voices and volume can drown out your voice. Help us to take this opportunity to remove ourselves from these distractions, and to listen to the gentle whispers of your message of love.**

FIRST CANDLE IS LIT

Leader It is easy for us to feel overwhelmed by the pressures of living and working with other people. As we reflect on the things which distract and upset us, we remember the way our Saviour and Brother, Jesus, regularly took time apart to be with his Father.

All **God of refreshment, as we spend time with you today, may we receive a sense of perspective about the issues which rise to trouble us. May we know that the Holy Spirit works within us to heal and refresh, to transform and renew.**

SECOND CANDLE IS LIT

Leader Sometimes we are afraid of silence; we can be afraid of hearing old voices reminding us of hurts and pains from the past; we can even be afraid of hearing new invitations to grow or step out or take a risk.

All **Creator and Healer, you know who we have been, who we are, and who we can become in your Love. Give us a deep sense of confidence so that we may come to you as trusting children, knowing that in your arms we shall receive understanding, acceptance, tailor-made challenges, and the power to grow more like you. Amen.**

THIRD CANDLE IS LIT

Retreat and advance – short talk 1

(Have ready a portable CD player and a CD with a modern song such as Robbie Williams' 'Millennium' although anything contemporary will do. Turn the CD on and play the first 30 seconds of the chosen song loudly and, WHILE IT IS PLAYING TRY TO TALK OVER THE TOP OF IT *– then switch off!)*

If I'd continued like that for a while you'd have probably switched off mentally and put your attention somewhere else! It takes so much effort to concentrate in the midst of noise and distraction, yet most of us spend our days surrounded by noise. Although we know that God can and does find ways of getting our attention using a whole range of ways, from the words of friends to the vivid images of a dream, it's hard for us to hear God when we are immersed in a noisy environment.

What does this 'audible noise' consist of?

• television, telephone, loud music
• machinery of one sort or another – lawnmowers, farm equipment, cars and motor-bikes, ticking clocks, roar of planes overhead
• people's voices – shouting, arguing, demanding, cajoling, discussing.

It's easy to imagine the benefits of moving away from this audible noise so we can hear God more clearly. But what about the noise that cannot be heard, the 'inaudible' noise of people's expectations, society's demands, financial pressures, health problems, or even relationship difficulties?

And there's a third sort of 'noise' as well – the 'internal noise' – not of our stomachs churning away to digest our meals or tell us we're hungry – but the internal noise of our thoughts. And with our thoughts come our fears and anxieties, our daydreaming about future possibilities, our preoccupation with the hundred and one things that have to be attended to . . . with our thoughts come old pains and hurts as well as new hopes and dreams.

Into the midst of our noise-saturated lives God speaks and says:

'Come to me, all you that are weary and are carrying heavy burdens,
and I will give you rest.'
Matthew 11.28

How do we come to him? Naturally we can come to him anytime, anywhere, but sometimes, particularly when we need to make a decision or when we have to face a crisis or even when we just need to remind ourselves that God is there for us, we come to him by making a retreat in the midst of our daily lives, setting aside time to listen to that still, small voice of God.

Retreat is an interesting word.

- *In military terms* it is linked to DEFEAT, a strategic or erratic withdrawal of troops after the enemy has got the better of them.
- *In politics* the term is being used more and more frequently to describe the meetings party members have at which policy is determined, issues are debated and the political team is brought closer, so it can present a united front to the rest of the country.
- *In real estate and commerce*, it is used to draw attention to a high quality (and high-priced) property which has a sense of remoteness and connection with the natural environment. Accommodation providers include the word 'retreat' in their advertising to accentuate qualities of luxury, tranquillity and rest.
- *In our faith journey*, the term retreat has always been used to mean setting aside time to spend with God, listening, resting, being strengthened or healed, challenged and encouraged. It is a time of recharging our spiritual batteries before we return to the routines of life. It does not have to be the preserve of clergy or those in religious orders; it can be of benefit to anyone who is serious about deepening their relationship with God.

It is also a time when faith communities can listen to God together to get a glimpse of possible ways forward, to heal old hurts, to share hopes and to be refreshed for new mission. Even a short time of retreat, such as this, provides an opportunity for God to work in our lives. It is a key part of growing in our faith and service, both as individuals, and together.

May this day provide you with a sacred space which you and God can share.

Retreat and advance – reflection sheet 1

Drawing apart for refreshment and renewal

From the Scripture passages below choose one that you feel comfortable working with. Read it slowly several times and let it speak to you about your situation. Take time then to 'talk' to God about what you are thinking and feeling, using words or drawing or even dance or movement!

Listen for God's reply . . . it may come now – it may come later – but it *will* come.

Jesus said: 'Come to me all you that are weary and are carrying heavy burdens, and I will give you rest.'
Matthew 11.28

Reflect on this Scripture and imagine yourself bringing your burdens to Jesus. Talk to him about your concerns and listen for his answer.

That evening, at sundown, they brought to him all who were sick or possessed with demons. And the whole city was gathered around the door. And he cured many who were sick with various diseases, and cast out many demons; . . . In the morning, while it was still very dark, he got up and went out to a deserted place, and there he prayed.
Mark 1.32–5

As you reflect on this Scripture, picture Jesus and the pressures that he faced. If Jesus needed to take time out with God, can you manage without doing the same?

For God alone my soul waits in silence,
for my hope is from him.
He alone is my rock and my salvation,
my fortress; I shall not be shaken.
Psalm 62.5–6

Retreat and advance – short talk 2

How many of you know the story about the committee whose members wanted to move the piano from one side of the church to the other – there was a great deal of opposition and so they decided that the only way to accomplish what they desired was to move the piano an inch a week towards the centre of the church – then move it across the aisle and then continue the gradual shift inch by inch until the piano was installed safely in its new position.

Sound far-fetched? Yet we all know that there is an element of truth in this story because as human beings we tend to resist change, and care has to be taken when new things are proposed.

There are times in our lives when we are called to move from the secure and familiar and to step out into the unknown . . . we are faced with having to make a change:

- when we leave school and go to another town for work or study
- when we make a choice of marriage or 'live-in' partner
- when we leave a job without another to go to
- when we are offered a leadership role and we wonder about our skills
- when we are faced with moving from our family home into a smaller unit
- when our bodies let us down and we have to adjust to impaired abilities.

In our spiritual journeys too there are times of being called to move from the secure and familiar and to step out in faith:

- when we begin to question and struggle with some of the things we read or hear about Christianity
- when we sense that there is much more to God than we have experienced so far, and we wonder where that 'more' may be found
- when we have the desire to go deeper, to get closer to God
- when the ways we have encountered God in the past no longer seem to 'work'
- when we start to read about other religions and wonder what makes Christianity unique
- when we lose someone close to us or experience some trauma and we wonder whether there is a God at all.

Jesus had to face all sorts of challenges, disappointments and decisions in his life and he made sure that he did what was needed to help him discern a way forward, to be equipped for the next stage of his ministry. Jesus went away on retreat, spending time in prayer to God. He went away on Quiet Nights rather than Quiet Days . . . the only way that he could get focused time with God.

Let's consider a few of the references to Jesus doing this:

- In Luke 6.12 Jesus spent the night praying to God before he chose his disciples.
- In Mark 1.35 Jesus went off to a solitary place to pray after the 'whole city' had gathered around his door demanding healing.
- In Matthew 14.23 Jesus went up a mountainside by himself to pray and when he came down he found his disciples had left so he went to them walking on the water.
- In Matthew 26.36 Jesus asked his disciples to watch with him while he went to a quiet place to pray – that place was Gethsemane.

Jesus went away to pray:

- *when he had to make a choice* – he went because he knew he needed WISDOM
- *when he was feeling drained and exhausted* – he went because he knew he needed RENEWAL and REFRESHMENT
- *when things were going well and he was in the midst of a busy ministry* – he went because he knew that he needed to KEEP HIS RELATIONSHIP WITH GOD STRONG and NOT FORGET THE SOURCE OF HIS LOVING HEALING POWER
- *when, in his humanity, he knew fear about the future* – he went because he knew he needed PEACE, COURAGE, AND INNER RESOLVE.

We can do what Jesus did and, like him, receive wisdom, renewal, refreshment, peace, courage, inner resolve, and a deepening of our relationship with God – and whatever else God desires to give us if we draw aside in prayer – in committed, purposeful, honest prayer . . .

By doing so we can be equipped for the next step, ready to move forward with God into the future, whatever it may hold. As King George VI said in his Christmas speech to the nation in 1939:

I said to the man who stood at the gate of the year, 'Give me a light that I may tread safely into the unknown.' And he replied, 'Go out and put your hand into the hand of God. That shall be to you better than a light and safer than a known way.'[20]

---

20 Minnie Louise Haskins (1875–1957), a retired lecturer at the London School of Economics, wrote these words as the introduction to a poem called 'The Desert' in 1908.

Retreat and advance – reflection sheet 2

Moving forward in our faith

Now during those days he went out to the mountain to pray;
and he spent the night in prayer to God.

And when day came, he called his disciples and chose twelve of them, whom he also named apostles.
Luke 6.12–13

Jesus had a crucial decision to make before he could move forward in his ministry.
He needed to discern the composition of his team and so he went apart to pray.

What decisions are you facing at the present time?

In confidence bring these to God, knowing that God understands the situation fully. Trust that a timely, wise and creative way forward can surface if you take the time to listen to God.

Read the passage of Scripture, Matthew 26.36–46

Jesus in the Garden of Gethsemane

Before Jesus could move forward to face the crucifixion,
before he could move forward to embrace the resurrection
that lay beyond that torment, he needed to pour out his heart to God.

If you are facing a 'Gethsemane' of your own, pour out your heart to God.
Your doubts and questions do not stop God from loving you; they can provide
a springboard which can propel you forward into an exciting new stage of your
faith journey and into a deeper relationship with God who will meet your need.

Crampons and crevasses
Opening worship

SENTENCE OF THE DAY

He drew me up from the desolate pit, out of the miry bog,
and set my feet upon a rock, making my steps secure.
Psalm 40.2

Leader O God of hospitality, we thank you for gathering us from our homes and heartaches, our challenges and our celebrations, so we may spend time with you in the sacred space of corporate silence.

All **We thank you for your sustaining love, present with us and all people, from the moment of conception to the moment of death when we return to you once more.**

FIRST CANDLE IS LIT

Leader Sometimes we find ourselves in awkward or even dangerous situations that threaten our confidence and undermine our faith. We need to hold on to you, but sometimes we feel as if you are far away.

All **Wise Leader on the expedition of our lives, help us to trust your experience and to recognize your guidance in the middle of our struggles and emptiness. May we come to know the reality of your daily provision for us and your desire to bring us to safe haven.**

SECOND CANDLE IS LIT

Leader As we come to spend this day with you, we long for rest, for glimpses of your grace and the courage to answer your invitation to intimacy.

All **May your Holy Spirit draw us closer to you this day, deepening our connection with you and reassuring us of your presence.**
May we be enriched for our ministry among those to whom you send us, whether family, friend, neighbour or stranger. Amen.

THIRD CANDLE IS LIT

Crampons and crevasses – short talk 1

I have never been mountain-climbing. Probably like many of you, I have seen such exploits on television and wondered at the motivation of those who are drawn to this form of recreation with its risk-taking and unexpected challenges.

But there have been times when the ground has given way under my feet, when I've found myself on a slippery slope or nearly lost my footing. I have been in danger of falling into symbolic 'crevasses' ; and I have been at risk of physical, emotional, relational and spiritual damage. A few examples:

- letting a stranger pray for me in a way that left me feeling spiritually abused
- being so overloaded with commitments that I burned out
- wanting a baby so much that I was in danger of becoming obsessed
- being depressed to the point of considering suicide . . .
- questioning my sexuality when involved with a gay male at university
- nearly getting killed on the road
- sitting with someone in tragic circumstances and finding my own faith challenged
- trusting someone who subsequently let me down.

We all have 'crevasses' in our own lives – times when we are brought face to face with our humanity, our frailty, with forces that are not of God, with unexpected moments of panic, with a sense of disconnection from all that has made sense to us in the past.

Some of you may still be recovering from a 'near miss' – something that took you to the edge of your faith and left you bruised and barely connected to the God who loves you.

There may be some of you here today who are in the middle of such a place of risk – a lonely, frightening place – a place of powerlessness and vulnerability and darkness – a place in which God seems distant and out of reach.

Hear the good news of Jesus Christ:
God is with us in the valleys as well as on the heights –
God is with us in the crevasses and on the mountain peaks.

None of us is alone. We are connected to God by the strong rope of Love that binds us in and to Christ. Nothing can separate us from the love of God (see Romans 8.38–9).

When we are unable to do anything to help ourselves, God sends 'rescuers' to help us, people who help and support us *from the outside in*.

- Sometimes there are literal rescuers who come alongside us and spend time with us, giving practical help or simply being present to comfort us.
- Sometimes there are people who are not even aware of the fact that they have been part of our recovery. For example, the singer-songwriter whose music touches your soul, the person whose chance remark you overhear, the stranger who smiles as you enter a shop.

These encounters remind us that we can't get out of a crevasse on our own; in fact, God encourages us to healthy interdependency, to the giving and receiving of support as we move through life.

One of the great lies of modern Western society is that the individual is self-sufficient, that we should be able to manage on our own. We are made for relationship not isolation and often we see this truth in times of tragedy, in the outpouring of sympathy and care which overrides conventional individualism.

But, however helpful other people are and however appropriate and timely their support, the best rescuer of all is the HOLY SPIRIT – the comforter who brings us to God *from the inside out*, who knows our needs and what is best for us.

As you spend time with God this morning, may God bring your awareness of the Third Person of the Trinity into focus. May the Holy Spirit's reality become clear in a new and comforting way this day.

Crampons and crevasses – reflection sheet 1

MAKING MY STEPS SECURE
a meditation on Psalm 40

All I can see above me
are the solid soles
of Your boots,
crampons jammed
into the unforgiving ice.

I dare not look below me
into the swirling mist
and dizzy depths
where death lies in wait
for the slip of the axe,
the slide of the toe.

I cannot see the next step
for the bulk of Your Being
fills my stinging eyes,
hiding the reality,
stark or shining,
of what lies ahead.

There is only this present moment:
a chiselled intensity redeemed
by single-minded trust;
a riveted togetherness
defying common sense;
a glimpse of eternity
etched into the mountainside
like a sculptor's prayer.[21]

Meditate on the following verses from the
Gospel of John

'But the Advocate, the Holy Spirit
whom the Father will send in my name
will teach you everything
and remind you of all that I
have said to you.'
John 14.26

When the Spirit of truth comes,
he will guide you into all the truth;
for he will not speak on his own,
but will speak whatever he hears,
and he will declare to you the
things that are to come.
He will glorify me,
because he will take what is mine
and declare it to you.
John 16.13–14

Using the process of 'holy reading'
(*lectio divina*)

slow reading, making connections,
'talking' to God, resting in God's love

pray with Psalm 40

Go for a walk and be alert for anything
which helps you connect with the theme
of safety or security

for example, a handrail by some stairs,
or traffic lights with a crossing signal.

Talk to God about your need for security
and safety.

---

21 First published in *Presence: Journal of Spiritual Directors International*, December 2005.

Crampons and crevasses – reflection sheet 2

Imagine that you are about to go on an exciting but scary adventure. For example:

- bungy jumping,
- rock climbing,
- a helicopter ride,
- white-water rafting,
- hot air ballooning,
- tandem skydiving.

Spend a few minutes getting in touch with what you would be feeling and thinking.

Then, in your imagination, allow yourself to approach the adventure, and, with Jesus by your side, enter fully into the experience.

Once the imaginative exercise is over, spend some time reflecting and journalling what happened for you, what you have learned about yourself and what you have learned about God.

Think of those key moments when people have helped you 'from the outside in'. You may like to list those who have supported you at pivotal times in your life. Then offer thanksgiving to God for each person.	When you consider the Trinity, with which Person do you feel most closely connected? Spend some time with that sacred Person, whether God, Jesus or Spirit, and let yourself be loved.

Crampons and crevasses – short talk 2

(Use an open discussion process with a whiteboard to help those participants who gather information visually. The sort of things people will identify, and/or which you can ensure are mentioned, are listed below.)

Starter questions

- What keeps you connected to Jesus ?
and/or
- What helps you stay aware of God's loving presence in your life?

Spiritual practices	regular prayer and Bible reading
	attending worship
	times of contemplation
	journalling
	reading spiritually helpful material
	music – listening or playing
	prayer walking
	sharing resources or experiences
	review of the day
	making a retreat
Connection with creation	many people feel close to God out of doors
Being with others	family gatherings
	parish groups
Creativity	as we deepen our relationship with God we often experience a growth in our creativity, not only in the sense of crafts, writing and music, but also in things like innovative solutions to dilemmas, or novel ways to proceed with a project.

Further questions

- What kept Jesus in close contact with his Father?
  (People's answers will probably focus on the one thing: prayer.)
- What sort of prayer?
  (Discussion may include some of the following –)
  Did Jesus pray for those whom he met each day? Too many to pray for individually probably – so he had to find a way to bring them to God –
  and he also needed restoration, infilling, ongoing support and closeness.

(Continue with the following short talk.)

It's likely that Jesus prayed contemplatively – a wordless 'being' with God in the deepest reaches of his soul and spirit – a heart-to-heart of divine proportions.

Thomas Keating quotes Gregory the Great's late sixth-century description of contemplation as 'the knowledge of God that is impregnated with love'.[22] Keating goes on to write:

> For Gregory contemplation is the fruit of reflection on God in Scripture and at the same time a gift of God. It is a resting in God. In this resting or stillness the mind and heart are not actively seeking Him but are beginning to experience, to taste, what they have been seeking. This places them in a state of tranquillity and profound interior peace. This state is not the suspension of all action, but the mingling of a few simple acts of will to sustain one's attention to God with the loving experience of God's presence.[23]

It isn't hard for us to imagine Jesus immersing himself in the love of God in this way, being nourished, prepared and re-sourced, not only for the demanding ministry of healing, but also for the risks and rigours of challenging unjust religious structures.

Although, from the sixteenth century onwards, contemplative prayer gradually came to be thought of as the preserve of the spiritual elite, today we are rediscovering that any one of us can pray in this way. We can engage in the ancient practice of *lectio divina* (sacred reading) – reading a small portion of Scripture, thinking about what it meant then and means to us now, talking to God about what we have discovered, and then, moving into contemplation, resting in God's love.

(If you would like more information about centring prayer and how it helps us move into contemplation, look at www.centeringprayer.com. You can either finish here or use this optional closing thought which reinforces the theme.)

Crampons are put on over the top of climbing boots – they are designed for a specific purpose – to keep the climber's footsteps firm on the mountainside. Perhaps contemplative prayer is like a set of crampons – helping our feet to stay on the path to fullness of life, so we may know profoundly that we are loved by God who, through the Holy Spirit, guides and sustains us on our journey.

---

22 Thomas Keating, *Foundations for Centring Prayer and the Christian Contemplative Life*, Continuum International, New York, 2004, p. 20.
   23 Ibid., pp. 20–1.

Crampons and crevasses – reflection sheet 3

How do you respond to the word 'contemplation'?

Talk to God about your feelings and thoughts in relation to 'resting in God'.

'Your Word is a lamp to my feet
and a light to my path'
Psalm 119.105

As you slowly read and reflect on this Scripture verse, let yourself imagine the path in front of you, the light which guides you and the One who holds you safely.

Then rest in God's love.

What other 'special footwear' might God want to give you to help you face an issue or meet a challenge?

- ballet shoes
- slippers
- work boots with steel toes
- flippers
- high-heeled evening shoes
- sports shoes with sprigs
- Wellington boots
- sandals, or baby shoes, or . . .

Bring before God your needs, listen for God's response – whether it comes now or later. Draw or write in your journal what you have discovered.

Which spiritual disciplines am I currently practising? For example, reading Scripture, centring prayer, journalling, fasting?

Which spiritual disciplines does God want me to include in my daily or weekly routine?

How might I stay connected to the One who loves me?

Rolling back the stone
Opening worship

'I have come in order that you might have life – life in all its fullness.'
John 10.10, Good News Bible

Leader We thank you Lord for bringing us here today, for gathering us together at this point in our own individual journeys so that we may spend time with you in corporate solitude.

All Generous God, you call us to abundant living. In you there are no half measures, no holding back of heart or hand for your nature is powered by the limitless creativity of Love.

May we open ourselves to your passionate plenty as we spend time with you this day.

FIRST CANDLE IS LIT

Leader Sometimes we find it hard to receive your love. Stones of hurt and grief and pride cover the well of life. But – little by little – you have been removing the gathered stones of the years, dismantling walls built by fears and failures.

All Master Builder, help us to see the work you have already done in our lives. You are making each one of us into a new creation, but sometimes the work is painful or confusing and we, in our childlike impatience, dare to wonder if you know what you are doing. Help us to see that you are rearranging the stones into patterns of promise and highways of hope.

May we trust in you as this transformation continues.

SECOND CANDLE IS LIT

Leader There will be times when we come to a particularly heavy or firmly fixed 'stone' and the thought of dislodging it fills us with anxiety. Letting go of the familiar, even if it is unpleasant, means making ourselves vulnerable as we become open to new ways of being.

All Loving Creator, give us the courage we need to let go of old habits and hurts and things that hold us back from growing in Christ. Forgive us when we resist your movement in our lives. Help us to know that nothing is impossible with you and that your desire is always to bring us to healing and holiness.

May we find our lives enriched as we learn from you this day. Amen.

THIRD CANDLE IS LIT

Rolling back the stone – short talk 1

The theme today is 'Rolling back the stone', and while we naturally think of the Easter story and the events of Easter Sunday, I actually want to start by referring to an Old Testament story from Genesis – a story going back to the time when Jacob was searching for a wife.

This is what the Scripture tells us *(read Genesis 29.1–3 from Reflection Sheet 1)*.

The story of course continues with the meeting between Jacob and Rachel, but what struck me forcefully was the image of the well being covered with a stone – a stone that had to be rolled away by the shepherds before their flocks could be watered.

And I began to think about our Christian journeys . . . and how in the early days of our lives as Christians we can easily be likened to these sheep – needing regular watering and nourishment. Often we are dependent on other Christians who may act as our shepherds, who work on our behalf, who make available to us opportunities to learn and grow in the faith . . . and we may be very aware of the leading of the Holy Spirit too at this time.

Part of your reflection before lunch may be to think about and thank God for such people – people who have been influential in supporting you in your faith walk – and to reflect on how the Holy Spirit spoke or touched your lives as you began your Christian walk.

But what happens as we go on along the path of faith?

Does God expect us to stay as sheep all our lives, dependent on the efforts of others to provide us with spiritual nourishment?

Well, in one sense yes – with Jesus as the Good Shepherd, we are all expected to follow Jesus and to maintain the focus on him, relying on him to guide us and protect us.

But there is another sense in which we are to keep growing and developing so we may in turn become shepherds for others . . .

In the process of growing in Christ, we gradually, perhaps painfully, let God have more and more room in our lives, and as we let God in so we are confronted with ourselves . . .

(Read the Scripture passage, Matthew 7.3–5, from 'The Message'.[24])

It's easy to see a smudge on your neighbour's face and be oblivious to the ugly sneer on your own. Do you have the nerve to say, 'Let me wash your face for you,' when your own face is distorted by contempt? It's this whole travelling road-show

---

24 Eugene H. Peterson, *The Message: The New Testament in Contemporary Language*, NavPress, Colorado, 1993, p. 25.

mentality all over again, playing a holier-than-thou part instead of just living your part. Wipe that ugly sneer off your own face, and you might be fit to offer a washcloth to your neighbour.

This version packs a bit of a punch, doesn't it? But in essence, Jesus is telling us to look at ourselves first – to be honest about ourselves before God.

Why? Is it so God can rebuke us and make us feel inadequate for having failed somewhere along the line?

No, being honest with ourselves and with God helps remove the stones piled over the well of Life and Love which God longs to make available to each of us. Being honest with God opens the channels of communication and liberates us from the bondage of our projections.

In the period up until lunchtime I invite you to use the first Reflection Sheet, which includes two Scripture passages and some questions for thought . . . feel free to take these sheets with you when you leave so you can have time to work through whatever God brings to mind today . . .

Rolling back the stone – reflection sheet 1

Then Jacob went on his journey and came to the land of the people of the east. As he looked, he saw a well in the field and three flocks of sheep lying there beside it; for out of that well the flocks were watered.

The stone on the well's mouth was large, and when all the flocks were gathered there, the shepherds would roll the stone from the mouth of the well and water the sheep, and put the stone back in its place on the mouth of the well.
Genesis 29.1–3

Who have acted as 'shepherds' for you so far on your Christian journey? Reflect on the part these people have played in your life . . .
on the effort they have exerted on your behalf and on the 'water' they have made available to you.

There may be things in your life, old hurts or griefs or resentments, which act like stones over a well preventing you from receiving all the life-giving 'water' which God wants you to have.

Acknowledging these old hurts and hindrances before God can help 'roll back the stone' . . .

Or perhaps there are 'hard-as-stone' attitudes which hinder your closer connection with others, maybe even with God.

With confidence in God's love for you, ask the Holy Spirit to show you any 'stones' which need rolling away.

'Why do you see the speck in your neighbour's eye, but do not notice the log in your own eye? Or how can you say to your neighbour, 'Let me take the speck out of your eye', while the log is in your own eye? . . . first take the log out of your own eye, and then you will see clearly to take the speck out of your neighbour's eye.'
Matthew 7.3–5

Rolling back the stone – short talk 2

The thought of becoming shepherds for others may be scary for some of us – perhaps for all of us – and yet that is surely how Christianity works, for we are told by Teresa of Avila, a teacher of the faith, a very down-to-earth mystic, that:

> Christ has no body now on earth but yours; no hands but yours, no feet but yours; yours are the eyes through which his love looks out to the world; yours are the feet with which he goes about doing good; yours are the hands with which he blesses now.[25]

So God calls us to grow as we follow Jesus, to take more responsibility for our own faith journeys and to help others along the way as a neighbour, or friend, or group leader or church minister.

Just as we try to teach our children to be independent, to gain the skills they need to manage without our constantly telling them what to do, so God hopes that we too will grow in knowledge and love of him to such an extent that we learn how to discern his will in a variety of ways . . . and as we grow he expects us to use our minds and our intuition and our talents . . . not to keep our intellect and our life-skills and experience locked away behind a stone . . .

As we grow in Christ, as we become shepherds for others, God moves us outside our comfort zones . . . for some of you coming here today was a step outside your comfort zone perhaps, something different and outside your experience . . . but those whom God calls he also equips for whatever task is given.

Let's consider the story of the raising of Lazarus. I'm sure that this task took Jesus to the outer limits of his comfort zone – to raise someone from the dead required of Jesus immense trust in the power of God. The task was made especially hard because Lazarus was a close friend, and the family's grief and anger was so raw . . . but Jesus faced the test, and even if there was struggle and effort in human emotional terms, he persevered because of the relationship of trust he had with the Heavenly Father . . . He knew he could count on God.

As God was faithful in the raising of Lazarus so he will be faithful with us as we seek to become more of who God created us to be . . .

And if you are worried that you may be asked to do or be something which makes you hesitant or fearful, remember the rolling away of the stone on the morning of the resurrection . . . nothing can match the power of God at work in the world, at work in your life.

Nothing is impossible with God.

---

25 James E. Kiefer, *Teresa of Avila*, www.justus.anglican.org/resources/bio/268.html

Rolling back the stone – a guided meditation
based on the raising of Lazarus

In preparation for this guided meditation, you are invited to get into a comfortable position, to take some slow, easy breaths and, when you are ready, to close your eyes. Remember that you don't need to struggle to make something happen. Just let images form if they will or notice an inner impression instead. Feel free at any time during the process to stop if you do not feel comfortable going on. Before we begin we pray:

> God who leads us from darkness into light,
> from bondage into freedom,
> send your Holy Spirit to surround, protect and guide us as
> we enter into the mystery of your work of grace in our lives.
> Amen.

So let us begin . . . take a minute or two to settle into silence and to allow your mind to become still. If distractions come, acknowledge them but set them 'on the back burner' for the time being, so you can pay attention to the present work of the Spirit in your life.

I invite you to imagine a cave . . . it could be one you have visited or one that you have heard of . . . but this cave is special to you and you alone . . . take some time to allow that cave to take shape for you. You realize that the entrance to this cave is blocked by a large stone – keeping you from seeing what is inside.

You become aware that this cave holds something which God wants to bring to life. Perhaps the cave holds a 'dead' talent which needs to see the light of day; or maybe there is a new area of ministry or service which 'scares you to death' and which you have thrust into the dark recesses of your mind; maybe there is something about yourself which you had thought was 'dead and buried' but which God wants to heal; perhaps the cave holds all sorts of new possibilities.

As you become aware of the cave, you also become aware that Jesus is standing outside with you. How do you feel as you realize you are not alone?

Jesus looks at you and there is immeasurable love in his eyes as he says: 'My beloved, roll away the stone.'

You look at the stone, then at Jesus, then back to the stone. You take a step towards it . . . How do you feel? What is going through your mind? You look at Jesus again, as if you hope he will remove the stone for you, but he remains loving you from a distance, knowing you must make this move for yourself.

If you are afraid of approaching the cave, turn and talk to Jesus about your fear. Then, if you feel safe, continue with the process . . . otherwise just stop at this point and take your feelings or questions to your reflection time this afternoon.

So . . . you begin to roll the stone away . . .

You are surprised how smoothly it slides away to reveal the entrance. You step back and wait with Jesus beside you to see what comes forth . . .

Once you have seen what emerges and have begun to explore it, you might like to talk to Jesus about what has happened. Together consider what it might mean for you; whether there is an invitation somewhere; what might be the next step.

Some years ago when I did this guided meditation with a group of people, I was surprised when the exercise became alive for me. Usually when I am leading others, I do not enter the scene fully myself so that I can better pay attention to the needs of the group, but this time was different.

As I looked at the entrance to the cave, I could see a dark tunnel receding into the hillside and turning a corner, but somehow I 'knew' there was a deep, steady source of light somewhere beyond my sight.

As I became aware of this, skipping out of the darkness, came a little girl aged around 5 or 6. She wore a frilly dress and her wavy hair was tied with ribbons. She was laughing and free and full of vitality.

When she got outside into the sun, she joined Jesus and me. We held hands and danced like kids in a fairytale.

In my imagination, I asked her name and she said, 'My name is Zoe,' which I subsequently learned means 'abundant life'. I asked her why she had come and she said simply, 'To help you learn to play again.'

I had always been a 'responsible child' and an even more responsible adult. Driven to achieve in order to gain approval, I had gradually shut down my capacity to play. This guided meditation opened up an invitation to get back in touch with that 'dead' part of myself and reassured me that Jesus would help me back to abundant life.

Rolling back the stone – reflection sheet 2

Then Jesus, again greatly disturbed, came to the tomb. It was a cave, and a stone was lying against it.
Jesus said,
'Take away the stone.'
Martha, the sister of the dead man, said to him, 'Lord, already there is a stench because he has been dead four days.'
Jesus said to her, 'Did I not tell you that if you believed, you would see the glory of God?'
So they took away the stone.
And Jesus looked upward and said, 'Father I thank you for having heard me. I knew that you always hear me, but I have said this for the sake of the crowd standing here, so that they may believe that you sent me.'
When he had said this, he cried with a loud voice, 'Lazarus, come out!'
John 11.38–43

As we grow in Christ,
as we become shepherds for others,
God calls us to take more responsibility for our faith journey and to move outside our comfort zones.

Perhaps God is calling you to do or be something for him which makes you hesitant, even fearful.

Talk to God about your fears and about taking risks for the sake of the Kingdom as you seek to grow in Christ.

Think about your life and the times when the seemingly impossible has happened and 'stones have been moved' to help you or others through a difficult situation.

Perhaps you are facing something at present which seems beyond resolution. Remember nothing is impossible with God.

Lift this situation to God in prayer and let the Holy Spirit guide you to deepen your trust in God's timing and purpose.

After the sabbath, as the first day of the week was dawning, Mary Magdalene and the other Mary went to see the tomb. And suddenly there was a great earthquake; for an angel of the Lord, descending from heaven, came and rolled back the stone and sat on it. His appearance was like lightning, and his clothing white as snow. For fear of him the guards shook and became like dead men. But the angel said to the women, 'Do not be afraid; I know that you are looking for Jesus who was crucified. He is not here; for he has been raised, as he said. Come, see the place where he lay.'
Matthew 28.1–6

Rolling back the stone – reflection sheet 3

REDEMPTION

Lord, this stone rolled
heavy over my heart
years long pains ago.
Although it makes it
hard to breathe,
I'm used to it, you know.

What will happen
if I start
to struggle under its weight?
Will I be crushed
or, cradled by Love,
be freed to stand up straight?

There's only one way
to know for sure
and that's to give it a try.
En-courage me, Lord,
Give me Your strength,
Without You I will die.

Ye . . . e . . . es!!

The world takes on
a whole new look
when I'm standing
straight and tall!
Thank You, Lord,
for Your amazing grace,
Your persistent Loving call.

You may like to use this passage of
Scripture as a meditation

Create in me a clean heart,
O God,
and put a new and right spirit
within me.
Psalm 51.10

Imagine that you are carrying
a load of stones –

let yourself identify each one

(you may like to draw yourself and label
the stones one by one)

then visualize yourself bringing these
stones to the foot of the cross.

What happens?

The foolishness of God
Opening worship

SENTENCE OF THE DAY
For God's foolishness is wiser than human wisdom,
and God's weakness is stronger than human strength.
1 Corinthians 1.25

Leader O God, who became vulnerable in Jesus, we thank you for calling us apart from our busy lives so that we can spend time with you in corporate solitude.

All **We thank you for the gift of this day and the opportunity it presents for us to reflect on the passion of Christ and the challenge of his servanthood.**

FIRST CANDLE IS LIT

Leader We live in the age of the knowledge economy, risking being swamped by a deluge of information, surrounded by insistent advertising, seeing world events through spin-doctors' eyes.

All **Your Way invites us to live as those who try not to be trapped by the values of our materialistic culture. Help us to seek your wisdom, rather than simply acquiring more and more knowledge.**

SECOND CANDLE IS LIT

Leader O God of the little ones of this world, your love at work can bring hope and healing if only your people have the courage to be your hands and heart, your voice of justice.

All **Help us, friend of the lost and lonely, to set aside the goals of the greedy and to accept the invitation to be fools for you.**
Amen.

THIRD CANDLE IS LIT

The foolishness of God – short talk 1

It seems a contradiction in terms, doesn't it? We are used to thinking of God as the highest expression of wisdom and yet in quite significant ways the full mystery of God's nature and purpose can only be approached through the concept of God's foolishness . . .

Foolishness of the incarnation

O wonder of wonders, which none can unfold:
The Ancient of Days is an hour or two old;
The maker of all things is made of the earth,
Man is worshipped by angels and God comes to birth.[26]

As Leech writes:

At the very core of the faith is the absurdity of the Word made flesh, God made small . . . so scandalous and so amazing is this truth that it is conventionally banished to the safe world of the Christmas card or crib. Christ is enclosed within the manger where he cannot grow up, teach, suffer or die, or rise again in this Peter Pan theology . . . until we recover the scandal and mystery, as well as the redemptive direction, of Christmas, we will not make much sense of Good Friday and Easter.[27]

In entering the human condition God became vulnerable; Love in its purest form became exposed to the worst excesses of human cruelty and violence and oppression.

Foolishness of the cross

How amazing that God should enter history so directly in the person of Jesus – but it is more amazing still that Jesus should 'empty' himself and make himself obedient to the most extreme form of death – crucifixion.
St Paul writes:

For the message about the cross is foolishness to those who are perishing, but to us who are being saved it is the power of God. For it is written, 'I will destroy the

---

26 Quoted in Kenneth Leech, *We Preach Christ Crucified*, Darton, Longman & Todd, London, 1994, p. 12.
27 Ibid, p. 12.

wisdom of the wise, and the discernment of the discerning I will thwart.' . . . Has not God made foolish the wisdom of the world? . . .

For Jews demand signs and Greeks desire wisdom, but we proclaim Christ crucified, a stumbling-block to Jews and foolishness to Gentiles, but to those who are called, both Jews and Greeks, Christ the power of God and the wisdom of God. For God's foolishness is wiser than human wisdom, and God's weakness is stronger than human strength.

(1 Corinthians 1.18–25)

The cross is described as 'insanity' (*moria* – 1 Corinthians 1.18f.). Yet we as Christians believe that Jesus endured crucifixion as one who was in the form of God . . . so Christians have dared to say that it was God who was crucified . . . God incarnate, Christ crucified hangs before us as a perpetual sign of the divine foolishness.

And so, as Christians, we dare to call the Friday before Easter Sunday, 'Good' Friday.

We dare to proclaim that in the crucifixion, God has somehow entered into the pain of the world, has taken that pain into himself, and has thus created the climate in which pain can be transformed into a means of healing and an impetus to struggle for a world in which pain is ended and death itself is swallowed up.

The crucified and suffering God, the 'man of sorrows and acquainted with grief' reveals the power of God in the midst of affliction . . . and provides a reassurance that God knows the reality of human pain and can sustain us through suffering, bringing us to a place of transformation if we let him.

We are challenged to allow ourselves to encounter the wounded and suffering God embodied in the crucified Christ.

The foolishness of God – reflection sheet 1

Use the *lectio divina* method of slow repetitive reading,
meditating, responding and contemplating
to help you focus on the mystery of the incarnation.

John 1.1–18 The Prologue to the Gospel of John

We read
(*lectio*)
under the eye of God
(*meditatio*)
until the heart is touched
(*oratio*)
and leaps to flame
(*contemplatio*)
Dom Marmion[28]

TENDER JESUS

Calm my fears,
Still my shaking;
dry my tears,
my anguish taking.
Touch my face
with light and peace;
may Your grace
my strength increase.

Religious silence
is silence that is
undertaken
as an act of worship.
Whether I hear God or
not makes
no difference.
Thomas Merton[29]

1 Corinthians 1.18–25: The foolishness of God

Read and reflect on the foolishness of God – the cross. You might like to write or draw something in your journal as God reveals more to you about the mystery of the cross.

---

28 Quoted in Thelma Hall, *Too Deep for Words*, Paulist Press, New Jersey, 1988, p. 44.
29 Quoted in *alive now! SILENCE*, Upper Room, Nashville, Nov./Dec. 1990, p. 32.

The foolishness of God – short talk 2

The foolishness of God in entrusting us with the Good News

Paul wrote in 1 Corinthians 1.26:

> Consider your own call, brothers and sisters:
> not many of you were wise by human standards,
> not many were powerful, not many were of noble birth.
> But God chose what is foolish in the world to shame the wise;
> God chose what is weak in the world to shame the strong.

In one sense, Christ could be said to be a 'fool', his entire life an act of folly. There is no sense in it by worldly conventional standards: his solidarity with outcasts, his polemic against the powerful religious leaders and the outwardly devout, all culminating in his death as a rebel and criminal.

We are called to be holy fools – to align ourselves with those people who have proclaimed the holy foolishness of God down the ages:
  the martyrs for the faith
  those who set aside wealth and status for work among the poor
  those who put themselves at risk in order to help others.

The holy fools were often nomads and pilgrims, always figures of the absurd who appeared particularly during periods of complacency in Church and society. St Francis was one such 'holy fool' setting aside the wealth and status to which he was born, behaving in a way that brought down the wrath of his father and the ridicule of his townspeople, yet following the way of Jesus by caring for the little ones, the outcasts, and seeking social justice and ecclesiastical reform.

A modern 'fool' for God was found on Good Friday 1994 – which also happened to be April Fool's day – Father Carl Kabat, dressed as a clown, hammered on a Minuteman III missile in North Dakota, an action for which he was sentenced to five years in prison.

In the Eastern Orthodox tradition the status of the holy fool is recognized liturgically and folly for Christ's sake is seen as an integral part of spirituality . . .

John Saward, writer of the authorit-
ative study[30] of folly for Christ's sake in
east and west, argues that the holiness of
fools shows itself most in their solidarity
with the outcasts of society – the *anawim*
(or little ones) – those on the margins –
the poor, the helpless, the handicapped,
the mentally ill, the ethnic minority, the
immigrant.

The holy fool is not content with
social work but enters into a deeper level
of identification with the wretched of the
earth, an identification that is sacrificial
and disconcerting for those around him.
We can think for example of Francis of
Assisi and the disbelief of his family as
he left the 'good life' behind, for a life
among the dispossessed of his day.

In contemporary life we can think
of the modern clown as someone who
is prepared to poke fun at the establish-
ment, to challenge institutions through
the use of humour and pathos – someone who aligns herself with the margin-
alized and the powerless.

There are Christian clowns in many centres who help us confront those values and
attitudes which reinforce oppression. Perhaps there are some among us who might
even have a sense of call to clowning, to this prophetic ministry expressed in a form
understandable to the person in the street.

Even though most of us might find this thought a bit frightening and would shy
away from a public expression of our beliefs using this medium, nevertheless we
are all called to be fools for the sake of Christ among those with whom we live and
work. Many Christians in fact suffer persecution today, not from tyrannical author-
ities or regimes, but from within their own households and neighbourhoods, simply
because they follow the One who models service before self in the midst of a Western
society which promotes individualism and acquisitiveness at enormous cost to the
majority of its inhabitants.

---

30 See John Saward, *Perfect Fools: Folly for Christ's Sake in Catholic and Orthodox
Spirituality*, Oxford University Press, Oxford, 1991.

The foolishness of God – reflection sheet 2

The call of God: Jeremiah 1.4–9

Reflect on the call of God in your life – its persistence, its challenge and its wooing.
As you have followed that call, how have you been aware of moving away from the
prevailing values of our culture?

Reflect on the image of the clown. Colour in, or write or use movement to enter into the paradox of clown as both prophet and positive fool.	Think about the people whose faith journeys you admire. What is there about them that could be described as 'foolish'? What is there about your faith journey which includes times as 'being a fool for Christ?'

Reflect on the 'hard saying'

If any want to become my followers, let them deny themselves and
take up their cross and follow me. For those who want to save their life
will lose it, and those who lose their life for my sake,
and for the sake of the gospel, will save it.
Mark 8.34–5

The foolishness of God – additional resources

(For leaders only – not for copying.)

GOD OF THE ABSURD

God of the absurd,
Creator of the feeding of pelicans,
the flight of pukeko,
the departing of baboons,
the singing of peacocks
and the hurrying of camels,
God of everything quaint, funny, incongruous,
you are the God who made me
and knows me through and through.

No one better than you
understands the contradictions
of my make-up, that mixture
of the sublime and the ridiculous
that is me. So, my loving Creator,
when I am experiencing the tension
of opposites, and am buried deep
in self-examination, please stop me
from taking myself too seriously.
Tune my ear to the laughter
of your universe,
and help me to understand it
as my own.
Joy Cowley [31]

---

31 Joy Cowley, *Aotearoa Psalms: Prayers of a New People*, Pleroma Christian Supplies, New Zealand, 2004. Used by permission.

Transition
Opening worship

SENTENCE OF THE DAY

The LORD will keep your going out and your coming in
from this time on and for evermore.
Psalm 121.8

Leader We thank you, gracious God, for bringing us here today, for gathering us together at this point in our individual journeys so that we may spend time with you in corporate solitude.

All As we come to you today, Lord,
we think about the transitions in our lives;
we think about the endings which we are facing,
we think about the task of letting go of people, of places,
of dreams, of hopes, of parts of ourselves . . .
May we be reminded of your faithful presence in our changes.

THE FIRST CANDLE IS LIT

Leader Light of the world, we find it hard to wander through the unmarked desert of uncertainty and emptiness which make up the landscape of our transition times. Fear and anxiety rise to meet us on the road; panic enters our hearts and minds as we face the darkness of the valleys of our lives.

All We need your guidance and the reassurance of your Holy Spirit to keep us safe on the path which you have prepared for us, even when we cannot see the way ahead.
Gift us with the grace of your Light to illuminate our path and warm our souls.

THE SECOND CANDLE IS LIT

Leader God of new beginnings, God of the butterfly and the rainbow, of autumn and spring, we thank you that with you there is always the promise of 'something more', a new song to sing, a new life to live in Christ.

All Creator God, help us to take the opportunities for fresh life and new beginnings which you make available to us, day by day.
Keep us open to the reality of the new things that you are doing in our lives and in our communities. Give us the courage we need to enter fully into the challenges ahead, so we may continue to grow into the fullness of Christ. Amen.

THE THIRD CANDLE IS LIT

Transition – short talk 1

When I was thinking about the word 'transition' the immediate association referred to a situation with which I am sure many of you are familiar: the moving of an elderly person from their own home into a rest home. However caringly such a transition is managed there is inevitable pain and dislocation which caregivers are powerless to prevent . . .

(If your group is made up of women who have had children, then the following may be a helpful inclusion or alternative to the above starting paragraph.)

Some of you might recall that the word 'transition' is the term used at the end of the first stage of labour, when the cervix is between 7 and 8cm dilated. This stage is described as a very stormy and challenging time as the woman is swept along by something beyond her control. She needs both emotional support and encouragement as she tries to concentrate and participate in the process of bringing a new person to birth.

(Ask those present to respond to this description and use the discussion to raise the issues which are referred to in the rest of this talk.)

Often we are companions of people in transition and, I believe, we can be more effective if we are prepared to identify and face our own transitions, learning from them the lessons which God would teach us.

This Quiet Day then has as its theme: 'Transition', so the first period before lunch provides the opportunity to reflect on the transitions in our own lives; the second period after lunch brings us to reflect on some of the transitions recorded in Scripture and how those speak to our situations today.

First let's think about our own transitions.

Some transitions can come about because of external changes in our circumstances; some of you might be familiar with the Holmes and Rahe[32] scale of Life Events ranking changes on a scale of difficulty with the death of a loved one top of the list – their well-researched theory, though not new, is borne out in the experience of many of us. We know that the more changes we face, good or bad, the more likely we are to suffer illness or fatigue, or to struggle emotionally.

Internal changes may be harder to identify and harder to attract support, for they may be invisible shifts in meaning and our sense of our own value and worth;

---

32 T. H. Holmes and R. H. Rahe, 'The Social Readjustment Rating Scale', *Journal of Psychosomatic Research* 11 (1967), pp. 213–18.

there may be the loss of a dream or an acknowledgement of ageing and the physical weakening that process can bring; there may be the development of a new talent or opportunity . . .

No matter what the triggering factor setting off the process of transition, all transitions tend to follow a similar cycle and as you read the process as described by Kathleen Fischer, perhaps you can be reflecting about your own current situation – about the transitions which you are now experiencing:

the process takes us from ending and relinquishment,
through emptiness and darkness,
to fresh life and new beginnings. *(repeat)*

This movement reminds us of the cyclical nature of all life: the pattern of the seasons, the waxing and waning of the moon, the ebb and flow of the tides.

Progress is not always swift and straight. There is compensation, adjustment and circling back. Our adult lives include many cycles of stability followed by periods of transition – for change is not simply a moment of our existence – but its pattern.[33]

The Bible is full of stories of transitions – people moving from one place to another physically, emotionally and spiritually. There are many examples of God's faithfulness in the midst of such transitions. I encourage you to use this time to reflect on whatever transition comes to you in prayer, as you offer this day to the guiding Holy Spirit.

---

33 Kathleen Fischer, *Autumn Gospel: Women in the Second Half of Life*, Paulist Press, New Jersey, 1995, p. 29.

Transition – reflection sheet 1

The process of transition takes us from ending and relinquishment, through emptiness and darkness, to fresh life and new beginnings. Progress is not always swift and straight. There is compensation, adjustment and circling back. Our adult lives include many cycles of stability followed by periods of transition – for change is not simply a moment of our existence – but its pattern.[33a]

Reflect on the changes and transitions in your life and ask yourself:

WHICH STAGE DO I FIND THE HARDEST?

The letting go ?

How hard is it for me to leave behind the past: places, people, position?

Is there something or someone I am holding onto which needs to be relinquished into God's care?

The darkness and emptiness?

How well do I manage in the desert where nothing apparently grows, no 'progress' seems to be made and time seems suspended?

What resources do I have to enable me to cope with the 'not knowings' of this period of uncertainty?

The new road ahead?

What is God saying to me about the way ahead – new paths, new chances of ministering, doing something 'risky' for the Kingdom, new ways of being myself?

May the Holy Spirit help me to identify anything which holds me back so I may offer these to God in prayer . . .

Scriptural references for meditation on the theme of 'Transition'

The story of Peter, his denial of Jesus and his restoration.

> John 13.36–8
> John 18.1–27
> John 21.15–19
> Acts 2

or

> The story of Ruth

33a Ibid, p. 29.

Transition – short talk 2

Faith tells us that this cycle of loss and gain is the crucible of transformation. During the immense struggle to embrace transition, what we most need is hope, and the confidence that, if we loosen our grip on the old, something worthwhile will emerge from the emptiness. It's not surprising that confidence literally means 'with faith' (Latin *con* (with) + *fidere* (to believe)).

Part of this hope comes from being able to understand the patterns of transition: the ending, the period in between, and the recognition of the new. Sometimes it seems that, in order for us to be free even to entertain the possibility of a new phase of life or work of grace, we have to leave the known behind. We may be called to take a 'step in faith' and to close a familiar, lucrative or interesting door *before* we have any idea of the shape a new ministry might take – the old has to be farewelled before we are free to welcome the new.

The process of reflection is invaluable as we enter transition stages of our life. We may undertake this process alone, for example by paying attention to our dreams and the insights which come during times of contemplative prayer and meditation; by committing something of our journey to paper so we can see how God is guiding us, comparing it with what we know of God's work in our lives up until this time. We can also benefit from companionship on this part of our spiritual journey, whether through regular meetings with a spiritual director or sharing with a wise prayer partner or mature group of fellow Christians.

Scripture is full of stories of transition – the ways in which Jesus dealt with the transitions he faced are particularly important as we seek to become more Christ-like in our daily lives. Think for example of the transitions he faced at the end of his earthly life:

- from being greeted as Messiah on Palm Sunday to being jeered at and abused before his trial
- from being followed faithfully by eager disciples to being betrayed and abandoned
- from knowing the fullness of God's love and relationship to feeling separated from God by the weight of human sinfulness
- from a public and painful death on the cross to the wonder of the resurrection.

May the Holy Spirit bring us to a deeper understanding of what Jesus relinquished; an appreciation of the gifts in the 'darkness' or 'desert' times; and a thankfulness for the new life which Jesus entered and which he seeks to share with us.

Transition – reflection sheet 2

Write your own story of transition.
Pray for the grace to see God at work in each of the stages:

- the letting go
- the waiting
- the welcoming of the new.

Take a large sheet of paper and, with crayons or felt-tip pens, make a diagram or a drawing of the significant transitions in your life.

When you have finished, take a 'Christ-colour' and let it move over the page, reminding you of the moments of grace and encounter with God at various stages of your life.

Talk to God about what you have discovered in this process.

TRANSITION

Take a walk and search
for symbols of transition
signs of the changing world
around you and within.

Paradox and pain
within the soul's rebirthing
are mirrored in the acorn,
the empty nest, the bud.

Cycles of yearning and of letting go
call us into growing
closer, God, to you.
For you alone are changeless.
In your Love and healing
alone do we find wholeness
and the blessed freedom,
gracefully to be.

What's in a name?
Opening worship

SENTENCE OF THE DAY
The name of the Lord is a strong tower; the righteous run into it and are safe.
Proverbs 18.10

Leader We thank you Lord for bringing us here today, for gathering us together at this point in our individual journeys so that we may spend time with you in corporate solitude.

All **Yahweh, we come from the 'busyness' of our daily lives into your peace. We carry all sort of names for you in our minds and hearts. As we spend time in silence and reflection, may you reveal more of yourself to us. May we come to know you more clearly this day.**

FIRST CANDLE IS LIT

Leader We thank you God of Creation that you delight in creativity and in the naming which follows. As Adam named the first fruits of your creation, so may we recognize and name the things which you are trying to bring to birth in us, new aspects of your creation given life and flesh through our being, new ways of being in closer relationship with you.

All **God of Challenge, sometimes we struggle with the changes that we must endure before you can bring new life to us, before we can take new life out into our families and communities. Help us to name our fears and problems honestly before you in prayerful expectation. May we gain more confidence in you this day.**

SECOND CANDLE IS LIT

Leader We thank you, God of Love, that you know each one of us by name and that each one of us is precious in your sight. Our Christian names are signs of our identity in you, our belonging to your family.

All **As we spend this day with you, may we come to know more deeply that you care about us as individuals and that we belong to you. May we hear you call us by name this day. Amen.**

THIRD CANDLE IS LIT

What's in a name? – short talk 1

A few years ago, there was a TV programme about the human body, and one episode showed the way children develop language. One particular scene followed a little girl as she went to the zoo with her mother.

The child was led to a small deer – like Bambi – the child's mother pointed to the animal and said gently: 'Deer'. The little girl looked at the creature and softly pronounced its name 'Deer'. And as she said the animal's name a change took place in her understanding – the animal moved from being simply a picture on a story book's page to a living reality.

That moment encapsulates the whole process of God's giving to human beings the power to name all creatures of the earth. Here was this child – a symbol of every living child – coming into relationship with creation by learning the names of each animal.

In human society the same process applies, for the first thing that we do in the Western world when faced with someone we don't know is to ask his or her name; the first thing a host or hostess does is to make sure the guests are introduced – that they know each other's name.

Using people's names helps us to *deepen our relationship* with them – think of how we choose our children's names, or whether we want to be called Nana or Grandma – or the way that, in tribal-based cultures, assigning a particular name can preserve an individual's affiliation to the tribe, strengthening identity and belonging through genealogical links.

And so it is with our relationship with God. We need to speak to God by name for our relationship to deepen.

Many of us, even if we've been Christians for only a relatively short time, will have become familiar with quite a number of names for God or ways of addressing God. We may, for example, have heard of the God of the Old Testament being referred to as Yahweh, Lord, Adonai, or Elohim. In the New Testament, with the coming of Jesus, we hear of God as Father or Gardener, and Jesus referring to himself as Shepherd, Light, Son of Man, Bread of Life.

Some of these names may already hold special meaning for us. For example, those of us who have grown up without a father, may find enormous help and comfort in the Father image of God. But, because of a hurtful or even damaging relationship with their earthly fathers, there will be some people who find the name 'Father' totally unhelpful, even repelling. That is why it is so important for each person to find a way of addressing God that breaks down barriers and helps us to approach God without fear. Jesus himself frequently used the term Father to speak of God and on one memorable occasion he used the term 'Abba' (our nearest equivalent would be something like Dad or Daddy) – an intimate, affectionate name showing the depth of his relationship with God and the closeness they shared.

Do you recall when Jesus used that term?

It was in the Garden of Gethsemane, when Jesus was faced with the horror of what lay ahead – the crucifixion; it was at that time that he needed to communicate on the most personal level with his Father . . . and so he called him Abba.

Do you have a special name for God – a name which shows something of your relationship with him?

While the Scriptures can offer us wonderful ways of naming God, we can also be surprised by God . . . offered new ways of looking at him which are part of our everyday lives. Here are two contemporary examples. The first is a poem using the tandem skydiver as an image of trust in Jesus.

A CONVERSATION WITH JESUS THE JUMPMASTER

Skydiving?
Me?
You must be joking?
No?
You *really* expect me to jump out of a plane?
What do you mean, 'Not alone?'
You would be there too?
So . . . I'd be yoked within your harness
        strapped in really tightly . . .
                enfolded in your strength
                dependent on your wisdom . . .
                        guided by your words
                        relaxed by your warm laughter . . .
                                empowered to take the risk
                                freed to soar and fly!
Promise you won't drop me?
Okay, then. I'll try!

The second example comes from an experience which occurred several years ago after I had been in England studying for a year. I returned home to New Zealand in time to attend my Diocesan Synod at an Anglican boys' school, near Hamilton. I was feeling sad and disconnected from my peers as I adjusted to being back in New Zealand. I looked for some time at the stained glass windows, thinking about some of the cathedrals I had visited while overseas.

In keeping with the boys who would attend services in this chapel, the windows showed Jesus as a youngster. There was something profoundly hopeful about the youth and innocence woven into the strength of his face.

As I looked closely at one of the windows depicting a teenage Jesus I found myself drawn to the shape and colour of the halo around his head. Its white and red sections reminded me of a lifebuoy – the sort of thing thrown to a drowning person to provide support – and all of a sudden I realized in a new and deeper way that Jesus was my *lifeboy* – that realization was an unexpected gift which sustained me through the transition of the next few months.

So may we all be aware of the new names for God that may come to us as gifts. As you work with some of the resources for reflection may the Holy Spirit guide you and help you explore who God is for you at this stage of your Christian journey.

What's in a name? – reflection sheet 1

Choose a passage for further reflection

When Jesus came into the
district of Caesarea Philippi, he
asked his disciples,
'Who do people say that the Son
of Man is?'
And they said,
'Some say John the Baptist,
but others Elijah, and still
others Jeremiah or one of the
prophets.'
He said to them, 'But who do
you say that I am?'
Matthew 16.13–15

He is named
Wonderful Counsellor,
Mighty God,
Everlasting Father,
Prince of Peace.
Isaiah 9.6

Going a little farther, he threw
himself on the ground and
prayed that, if it were possible,
the hour might pass from him.
He said, 'Abba, Father, for you
all things are possible; remove
this cup from me; yet, not what
I want, but what you want.'
Mark 14.35–6

'I am the true vine, and my
Father is the vine-grower . . .
I am the vine, you are the
branches.
Those who abide in me and I in
them bear much fruit, because
apart from me you can do
nothing.'
John 15.1, 5

Jesus said:
'I am the light of the world.
Whoever follows me will
never walk in darkness
but will have the light of life.'
John 8.12

Can a mother forget her
nursing-child, or show no
compassion for the child
of her womb?
Even these may forget,
yet I will not forget you.
See, I have inscribed you
on the palms of my hands.
Isaiah 49.15–16a

Sheet of Scripture reproduced to accompany Quiet Day.

What's in a name? – short talk 2

When we read Scripture we might have been conscious of people who have experienced a change of name:

Abram becomes Abraham meaning 'father of many'
Sarai becomes Sarah meaning 'princess'
Simon becomes Peter meaning 'the rock'

This name change may precede a new call . . . a new challenge or a new phase of commitment . . . but always a deepening of the individual's relationship with God. In Peter's case it was a call to be the rock on which the Church was to be built, even though at the time Peter had no idea that Jesus would call him to that role.

But what about the changing of names today – does God still offer us a new identity or perhaps a chance to reclaim some hidden parts of ourselves?

We know that there are times in our culture when people change their names to indicate an important transition in their lives:

- until recently, nuns would take a new name as they made their final vows
- many women still take their husband's surname when they marry
- some people choose to be known by a nickname or even change their name by deed poll to make a strong statement about their identity
- some people who have grown up with European names are now choosing a name from their own culture as a way of reclaiming their heritage.

God may not want us to change our Christian names (there will come a time when a new name may be revealed – Revelation 2.17, which speaks of believers receiving a white stone on which will be written a new name), but God may want to help us change some of the names we give ourselves, particularly any limiting labels with which we may struggle . . .

This invitation is captured beautifully in these words from Isaiah which will be available for you to use after the guided meditation if you wish. Isaiah writes:

And you shall be called by a new name
that the mouth of the LORD will give . . .
You shall no more be termed Forsaken . . .
but you shall be called
My Delight Is in Her . . .

Isaiah 62.2b,4

A guided meditation on the Scripture passage
John 20.11–16a

Remember that you are free to participate in this guided meditation or not as you prefer – not everyone finds using their imagination easy, so don't struggle to make anything happen – let images form if they will – or simply become aware of an inner sense of what is happening, a sort of knowing without images or words.

I am going to read the Scripture passage through first to reacquaint you with the story – then I will guide you through it. When we reach the stage where Jesus turns to face Mary, you will be invited to let the meditation unfold as seems best for you and to let it come to a natural conclusion. Then, when you are ready, move into the rest of the afternoon's reflection time.

I invite you to put aside anything which you are carrying – just put it on the ground or beside you so your hands are free. You may like to close your eyes so you are not distracted by other people; just take a few easy breaths and begin to relax.

Let us begin with a prayer:

Loving God who created us with imaginations, we offer this time to you and pray that the Holy Spirit will be present to guide and protect us and help us to draw closer to you. Amen.

I'll read the story through:

But Mary stood weeping outside the tomb. As she wept, she bent over to look into the tomb; and she saw two angels in white, sitting where the body of Jesus had been lying, one at the head and the other at the feet.
They said to her, 'Woman, why are you weeping?' She said to them, 'They have taken away my Lord, and I do not know where they have laid him.'
When she had said this, she turned round and saw Jesus standing there, but she did not know that it was Jesus. Jesus said to her, 'Woman, why are you weeping? For whom are you looking?' Supposing him to be the gardener, she said to him, 'Sir, if you have carried him away, tell me where you have laid him, and I will take him away.'
Jesus said to her, 'Mary!'

I invite you now to let yourself enter that scene – to picture the tomb, the stone rolled aside, the entrance looming dark before you. (Take some time to let this emerge.) When you are ready, place yourself in the scene – so that you can see what

Mary sees. You look inside the tomb, bend down and carefully, hesitantly, step into the darkness . . .

But it is not as dark as you had expected, for there are two bright beings taking shape before you – in the place where you had expected Jesus' body to be lying, there are two angels in white. How do you feel as you see this sight?

What, if anything, do they say to you?

What, if anything, do you say to them in return?

Let yourself drink in the light which the angels bring – let yourself be warmed as the darkness is melted by their brightness – let something of the love which energizes them, touch your tears.

Then, when you are ready, turn away from the scene inside the tomb and look back outside – a shadowy shape emerges from the bleakness of the morning – the person asks you 'Why are you weeping?'

Let your response take voice . . . let the things which are difficult to bear be revealed to this kind and gentle Presence . . .

As you come to the end of your story, you become aware of the Living One, Jesus, who stands in front of you – and you hear Jesus call you by name . . .

What's in a name? – reflection sheet 2

. . . and you shall be called by a new name
that the mouth of the LORD will give.
You shall be a crown of beauty
in the hand of the LORD,
and a royal diadem in the hand
of your God.
You shall no more be termed
Forsaken,
and your land shall no more be
termed Desolate;
but you shall be called
My Delight Is in Her,
and your land Married.
Isaiah 62.2b–4

As you reflect on the passage above, let the Holy Spirit bring to mind any destructive labels or unhelpful adjectives which have, over the years, somehow become part of your life. Let yourself hear the new names that God longs for you to hear, names which say something about hope, peace, joy and strength.

You shall be called by a new name

....

....

You shall no more be termed

....

....

but you shall be called

....

....

Greed and grace
Opening worship

SENTENCE OF THE DAY

The law indeed was given through Moses; grace and truth came through Jesus Christ.
John 1.17

Leader   We come as we are Loving God
to spend time in corporate solitude
and to rest in you today.

All   **We bring with us all sorts of things
that occupy our minds and take our energy:
hopes and fears,
tasks and tears,
the trivial and the overwhelming details of each day.**

FIRST CANDLE IS LIT

Leader   Help us to approach this time with confidence,
knowing that you desire our healing and our holiness.

All   **Help us to begin to look at what we hold tightly,
at what we are afraid to relinquish into your Love.**

SECOND CANDLE IS LIT

Leader   May we be given a glimpse
of the riches of your grace,
made accessible through the One
in whom your Love took flesh and form.

All   **As we step aside from the busyness
which clouds our vision of your glory,
may your Holy Spirit
reveal to us the depth and breadth
of your Love for us
and for the whole of your creation. Amen.**

THIRD CANDLE IS LIT

Greed and grace – short talk 1

(To start this Quiet Day either read Luke 12.16–21 or the following summary of a contemporary children's story by Julie Sharp, 'Oliver Cornwell'[34] *– this book is based on the biblical story of the merchant who gathered so much grain into his barns but neglected his spiritual and ethical life.)*

Oliver Cornwell built an empire from corn – cornflakes sold at Sainsbury's, corn-on-the-cob for Macdonalds, and cornchips sold at Marks and Spencers; he sold corn oil and even jewellery made from corn. He stored all his considerable wealth in many different banks *(you can insert details of different banks' names if you want to!)* and was rich enough to travel the world *(again you can insert a variety of destinations and expensive activities, such as ballooning in Turkey or kayaking in the Antarctic!)* and to pay for front row seats at the theatre.

Oliver Cornwell hired servants to take care of absolutely everything from ironing his newspaper to choosing what he should wear each day. He spent thousands on little luxuries for himself but didn't think about anyone else, keeping the poor from his door with guard dogs.

One day he planned a huge party for his rich neighbours. Satisfied with all the things he had put in place for the event, he went upstairs with his evening snack on a golden tray: cornflakes and cream, of course.

But – one gluttonous mouthful later he started to cough and splutter and finally choked – Oliver Cornwell was dead!

When you saw the word 'greed' written as part of the theme for this Quiet Day, you may have started thinking about the sorts of things that landed Oliver in strife – the way we can so easily make a focus of material things and the status which money can bring with its power and influence . . . indeed much of our Western culture has that focus and none of us is immune to consumerism and the values associated with it.

Sometimes we may find that there is another form of greed operating – I'm sure you've all heard the expression 'knowledge is power', referring to the situation in which those who have information, understanding, knowledge or access to it can act as gatekeepers, preventing other people from growing and learning more.

This has certainly happened in the Church as a whole over the centuries – and it operates in any institution or system, including families, whenever people refuse to

---

34 Julie Sharp (text) and Maria Lee (illustrations), *Oliver Cornwell*, Hunt & Thorpe, Hampshire, 1998.

share their talents and skills with those around them. And there may be issues in your past which you can bring to God for healing in this area.

But what I am thinking of is another application of the word 'greed' – one that may help us connect with parts of ourselves that we may seldom visit or own.

What I am talking about are those parts of our lives which we prefer to keep to ourselves, to hold close, sometimes without realizing we are doing so. Our God is the Creator – a God who desires to sing a new song in each of our hearts. Yet sometimes we hinder God's creativity because we are holding on so tightly to something which we hold dear, that we are not free to receive what God longs to give us.

Without realizing what we are doing, we lay up for ourselves 'treasures on earth'
– not just goods and chattels, money and real estate: we can become attached to
particular personal habits,
particular people,
particular jobs or functions in an organization or a church,
even particular ways of praying and worshipping.

Without realizing it,
we can become possessive of these parts of our lives,
we can resist God's invitation to let some of these things go
and we can stop the release of energy needed for our spiritual growth.

Why do we hold on so tightly to our possessions, to people, to information?

The Bible recognizes this tendency in us and provides an insight into what might contribute to this behaviour in the Parable of the Talents found in Matthew 25. If we look especially at the last person – the one with *the one talent* we are nearer to understanding something about the reason for our reluctance to give up what we have:

'I was afraid, and I went and hid your talent in the ground . . .'

GREED EMERGES OUT OF FEAR

fear of losing something or someone precious
fear of losing whatever we have been using for our security
fear of being abandoned and having nothing to sustain us

The effect on us of this other, often hidden side of greed, can be represented by the symbol of the closed fist.

Can I invite you to close your fists tightly and to feel what that is like as you hold the tension for a few moments.

Now gradually let your fists become relaxed and become aware of the difference between the two states: tension and relaxation.

Even after a few seconds you'll probably have realized that, if held for too long this position can have an effect on the whole body:

* you might be aware of tightness
  and the draining of emotional and spiritual energy,
* you might recognize that keeping things to ourselves limits our ability
  to respond and relate to others; it can hamper our prayer life
  and restrict freedom to express our joy in God.

We hold on tightly because we are afraid of letting go . . . and particularly because we are reluctant to relinquish control over our lives, however illusory that control might really be.

But God does not want us to be afraid.

God desires to help us grow more like Jesus and to be set free of all that holds us back from a deeper relationship with him through the Holy Spirit . . .

May your time of reflection this morning help you to move closer to the Lord who loves you and calls you to his side.

Greed and grace – reflection sheet 1

Matthew 6.19–24
Treasures in heaven

Use the *lectio divina* method of slow repetitive reading,
meditating, responding and contemplating
to help you focus on where your priorities currently lie
and what God might be saying to you about this.

We read
(*lectio*)
under the eye of God
(*meditatio*)
until the heart is touched
(*oratio*)
and leaps to flame
(*contemplatio*)
Dom Marmion[35]

Questions for reflection

- What am I afraid to let go of? In what do I put my trust, my security?
- What am I keeping to myself which God may be inviting me to share with others?
- What habits may be hindering my spiritual growth?
- What material things am I attached to?

---

35 Quoted in Thelma Hall, *Too Deep for Words*, Paulist Press, New Jersey, 1988, p. 44.

Greed and grace – short talk 2

Not so very long ago I received an unexpected gift. A lady had died – I hadn't spoken to her for several years but, in her will, it was clear that she had wanted to leave me some money.

Naturally I was surprised and a bit taken aback. I wrestled with feelings of unworthiness, wondering why I was receiving this generous and in my opinion undeserved gift. I felt guilty because I had not been in recent contact with her and had neglected to pay her the attention she deserved. But as I reflected and spoke to one of her close friends, I came to see that she left me some money just because she loved me, in spite of my failures in care and contact. I knew that I was participating in a gracious and loving sharing of her wealth.

It's a bit like that with God and with grace –

we do not earn it
it is not dependent upon how many good works we perform
we can only learn to receive it.

(You may want to ask participants if they want to share any similar stories of grace and/or read the following story of the Prisoner's conversation with God.)

Piri Thomas[36] in his book, *Down these Mean Streets*, has a moving scene in which a prisoner is speaking:

I went back to my cell the night before my hearing.
I decided to make a prayer.
It had to be on my knees . . . I couldn't play it cheap.
So I waited until the thin kid was asleep.
Then I quietly climbed down from my top bunk and bent my knees.
I knelt at the foot of the bed and told God what was in my heart.
I made like he was there in the flesh with me.
I talked to him plain . . . no big words, no almighties . . .
I talked with him like I had wanted
to talk to my old man so many years ago.
I talked like a little kid and I told him of my wants and lack,
of my hopes and disappointments.
I asked the Big Man . . .
to make a cool way for me . . .
I felt like I was someone that belonged to somebody who cared.

---

36 Quoted in William J. Bausch, *A World of Stories for Preachers and Teachers*, 23rd Publications: Mystic, Connecticut, 1998, pp. 316–17.

I felt like I could even cry if I wanted to,
something I hadn't been able to do for years.
'God,' I concluded, 'maybe I won't be an angel
but I do know I'll try not to be a blank.
So in your name and in Cisto's name, I ask this. Amen.'
A small voice added another amen to mine.
I looked up and saw the thin kid,
his elbows bent, his head resting on his hand.
I peered through the semidarkness to see his face . . .
No one spoke for a long while.
Then the kid whispered,
'I believe in Dios also. Maybe you don't believe it,
but I used to go to church
and I had the hand of God upon me.
I felt always like you
and I feel now warm, quiet and peaceful
like there's no suffering in our hearts.'
What is he called, Chico, this what we ask for? I asked quietly.
'He's called Grace by the Power of the Holy Spirit,' the kid said.

It's hard for most of us to be open to the unconditional love of God; we are so accustomed to putting conditions on our own loving/relating to people: we are so accustomed to recognizing the conditions others place on their loving

I'll accept you if you do things my way
I'll help you provided that . . .

It's hard for us to take on board the reality of God's love for us
It's hard for us to believe the undeserved, unmerited, unrepayable favour graciously offered to us . . .
So many Christians try to earn God's favour – many get caught up in a performance trap that exhausts them – they become POW's (Prisoners of Works). Instead of feeling that they've earned enough 'brownie points' working for God – many are left feeling exhausted.
We do not have to do anything to earn God's love – it is unconditional . . . and for each person – every single one of us – you and me.
May the time of reflection this afternoon help you connect freely with the grace of God – grace like a river, flowing strong and true.

Greed and grace – reflection sheet 2

The grace of God
John 1.14–17

Reflect on the grace of God in your life – its unexpectedness, its capacity to surprise and delight, its timing . . .

How have you seen grace at work in people 'outside' the Church, people who may not consider themselves 'religious'?

An early mnemonic for *grace* reads

God's
Riches
At
Christ's
Expense

Reflect on this and then make up a mnemonic of your own which has special meaning for you in relation to God's grace.

What are the sacraments?
They are the outward and visible sign of inward and spiritual grace, given by Christ to the Church.

What is grace?
Grace is God's freely-given love for people, forgiving sins, enlightening minds, stirring hearts and strengthening wills. Through grace we are given the strength to live as loving sons and daughters of God.
New Zealand Prayer Book[37]

THE WOMB OF GOD

I dwell within
the womb of God
being within Being,
hearing attuned to Heartbeat,
learning instructed by Wisdom,
growing dependent on Grace,
trusting nurtured by Love.
Within the womb
of God I dwell . . . secure.

---

37 *New Zealand Prayer Book*, Genesis, Christchurch, new edition 2002, p. 932.

Greed and grace – additional resources

(For leaders – not for copying.)

Dear God
I am so afraid to open my clenched fists!
Who will I be when I have nothing left
to hold on to?
Who will I be when I stand before you
with empty hands?
Please help me to gradually open my hands and to discover that
I am not what I own,
but what you want to give me.
And what you want to give me is love,
unconditional, everlasting love.
Amen
Henri Nouwen[38]

Dear God
I so much want to be in control,
I want to be master of my own destiny.
Still I know that you are saying:
'Let me take you by the hand and lead you.
Accept my love
and trust that where I will bring you,
the deepest desires of your heart will be fulfilled.'
Lord, open my hands to receive your gift of love.
Amen
Henri Nouwen[39]

Cheap grace is grace without discipleship, grace without the cross, grace without Jesus Christ, living and incarnate.

Costly grace is the treasure hidden in the field; for the sake of it a man will gladly go and sell all that he has. It is costly because it costs a man his life, and it is grace because it gives a man the only true life.
Dietrich Bonhoeffer[40]

---

38 Henri Nouwen, *With Open Hands*, Ave Maria, Indiana, 1995, p. 21. Used by permission.

39 Ibid., p. 28.

40 Dietrich Bonhoeffer, *The Cost of Discipleship*, MacMillan, New York, 1963, p. 47.

Choose life!
Opening worship

SENTENCE OF THE DAY
'I have come in order that you might have life – life in all its fullness.'
John 10.10, Good News Bible

Leader   We thank you Lord for bringing us here today, for gathering us together at this point in our individual journeys so that we may spend time with you in corporate solitude.

All   **As we come to you Lord, we think about our lives and the choices we make. If everything is going well in our lives, then we find it easy to make the hundreds of choices which occur in a given week; but if we are tired or stressed or depressed, decision-making can be a burden and we worry about the 'rightness' or 'wrongness' of our choices, long after they have been made. Help us Lord to lean on you whenever we feel swamped by a deluge of choices.**

FIRST CANDLE IS LIT

Leader   O God, our guide, there have been times when the choices we have made have led us away from you, when we have had other goals and sought after other gods – gods like money or status or security.

All   **We know that you are the God who constantly calls us back to yourself; you have made us for yourself and our hearts are restless until they rest in you. Time after time, you give us the chance to turn from all that weakens our spirits so we may be nourished by your love. Help us Lord to be aware of your patient, persistent call to turn towards you minute by minute, day by day.**

SECOND CANDLE IS LIT

Leader   O God our healer, help us to deepen our trust in you and your work in our lives. You promise us a richness and depth of living that is beyond the world's understanding. You promise us your presence to sustain and strengthen us.

All   **Help us Lord to take hold of the opportunities which you prepare for us, to make choices which affirm our willingness to follow in your footsteps even if that means going against popular opinion and practice. Help us to discern when we need to make the difficult choice of letting go of something or someone, so you may work in their lives. May our choices honour you and be a blessing to others. Amen.**

THIRD CANDLE IS LIT

Choose life! – short talk 1

(Have ready the following visual aids: 3 small cups and a hazelnut; 2 question marks, cut out of card, each about 15cm (6in) high, one black and one white; varieties of packet soup, sauce or casserole mixes or whichever other similar ordinary food items you have available. These are to remind us of the range of choices available to us, even in a simple daily activity such as grocery shopping. Use these according to the directions given in brackets in the body of the text.)

Choice is a funny thing – however much we have, we always seem to want more . . . many of us remember growing up with limited options in terms of the food that was available for example – I can still remember having ham sandwiches for what seemed my entire secondary school career!

(Set out the cups under one of which you have hidden the hazelnut.)

The basis on which we make decisions becomes more complex as we develop. As little children we might recall the game of trying to find something hidden under a cup. *(Demonstrate the game with one of the participants.)* At this stage of our lives, decision-making is haphazard, based on guesswork and hampered by the underdeveloped intellectual capacity of a young child. As we enter adolescence our ability to make more complex decisions increases with our intellectual, social and emotional development. *(Place the black and white question marks on the floor in the middle of the group.)* But the idealism of adolescence can lead individuals to choice-making which is 'black and white' with little room for compromise.

'Magical' thinking links good outcomes with external events (I'll pass my exams if that light turns green before I get to it!). Although understandable in children's thinking, it becomes problematic if it persists into adulthood, and finds expression in an openness to the concepts of superstition and 'luck' influencing our decisions.

By the time we reach adulthood, although our ability to make choices has hopefully matured, we are faced with such a plethora of alternatives *(scatter the unopened packets onto the floor)* that it can be really hard to work out which choice to make, whether we are purchasing our weekly groceries or choosing a car or computer . . . even a life partner!

But the choices which we want to concentrate on today concern those which affect our faith journey. If we look back over our lives, we can probably see that there are definite times when we've made choices which have taken us further away from God just as there have been times when we have made choices which have taken us closer to God.

86

One of the reflections available today involves drawing a timeline and putting on it, above and below the line, those significant moments of choice.

I distinctly remember one such time for me when I had left home to go flatting, as many young people do. The flat happened to be directly opposite the local Anglican church, but I didn't cross the church's doorstep for the entire year I lived there! It was a deliberate choice – and part of the reason had to do with the lifestyle I was living at the time.

If you feel you need to, you can talk to God today, acknowledging your times of turning away. Be assured that God's forgiveness is freely and abundantly yours.

As you reflect this morning, you may be surprised to see how perhaps several times in your life, you have been brought back into an awareness of your relationship with God or you have taken steps to deepen your relationship in response to the working of the Holy Spirit in your life, whether you recognized it as such or not.

Being aware of God's patient and persistent calling of us back to himself can be an immense source of encouragement – not only for each of us as individuals, but also for our families, particularly those whom we love but who may at present have made choices which have moved them away from God (or so they and we might think – although in truth none of us is ever out of God's reach).

> Where can I go from your spirit? Or where can I flee from your presence?
> If I ascend to heaven, you are there;
> if I make my bed in Sheol, you are there.
> If I take the wings of the morning and settle at the farthest limits of the sea,
> even there your hand shall lead me, and your right hand shall hold me fast.
> *Psalm 139.7–10*

As you enter the quietness and reflect on the theme of 'Choosing life', may you be encouraged by what God *has already done in your life* to bring you to this point.

Choose life! – reflection sheet 1

Read slowly through these quotations and let one become a focus for your meditation

See, I have set before you today life and prosperity, death and adversity. If you obey the commandments of the LORD your God that I am commanding you today, by loving the LORD your God, walking in his ways, and observing his commandments, decrees, and ordinances, then you shall live and become numerous, and the LORD your God will bless you in the land that you are entering to possess . . . I call heaven and earth to witness against you today that I have set before you life and death, blessings and curses. Choose life so that you and your descendants may live, loving the LORD your God, obeying him, and holding fast to him; for that means life to you . . . *Deuteronomy 30.15–16, 19–20a*	But you, O Israel, my servant, Jacob, whom I have chosen, the offspring of Abraham my friend; you whom I took from the ends of the earth, and called from its farthest corners, saying to you, 'You are my servant, I have chosen you and not cast you off; do not fear, for I am with you, do not be afraid, for I am your God; I will strengthen you, I will help you, and I will uphold you with my victorious right hand.' *Isaiah 41.8–10*
'You did not choose me, but I chose you. And I appointed you to go and bear fruit, fruit that will last.' *John 15.16a*	'. . . choose this day whom you will serve . . .' *Joshua 24.14–24*
For what has been – thanks! For what shall be – yes! *Dag Hammarskjöld*[41]	But you are a chosen race, a royal priesthood, a holy nation, God's own people, in order that you may proclaim the mighty acts of him who called you out of darkness into his marvellous light. *1 Peter 2.9*

41 Quoted in Margaret Pepper (ed.), *The Macmillan Dictionary of Religious Quotations*, Macmillan, London, 1996, p. 14.

Reproduced for use on Quiet Day.

MOMENTS OF CHOICE WHICH TOOK ME 'NEARER TO GOD' . . .

10

1

BIRTH . . . . present day

1

10

MOMENTS OF CHOICE WHICH TOOK ME 'FURTHER AWAY FROM GOD' . . .

Choose life! – short talk 2

(This talk is interactive – using a whiteboard to record responses to the question 'What do you think abundant life means?' the leader ensures that the following key points are covered, either raised from the group or offered by the leader.)

Fruits of the spirit Galatians 5 – love, joy, peace, patience, kindness, goodness, faithfulness, gentleness and self-control

Less worrying

Freedom of choice we are not forced to make choices based on fear, or based on keeping up appearances, or because we try to keep our anxiety at bay by keeping control

Openness to new opportunities

Contentment whatever our situation

Improved relationships and reconciliation

A deeper awareness of the reality of God's action in our lives

Different attitudes to such things as use of money, choice of entertainment, the plight of the poor

Greater creativity

(When the discussion has come to a close and if you sense that it is appropriate for your particular group, move into guided meditation using the John 10.10 Scripture: 'I have come that you might have life – life in all its fullness.')

A guided meditation on the Scripture passage John 10.10

Remember that you are free to participate in this guided meditation or not as you prefer – not everyone finds using their imagination easy so don't worry about trying to make anything happen – let images form if they will – or simply become aware of an inner sense of what is happening, a sort of knowing without images or words.

 You may like to close your eyes so you are not distracted by other people; just take a few easy breaths and begin to relax. Let us pray:

Loving God who created us with imaginations, we offer this time to you and pray that the Holy Spirit will be present to guide and protect us and help us to connect more deeply with the abundant life which you offer to us all. Amen.

(Read the Scripture through twice, slowly.)

Jesus said: 'I have come that you might have life – life in all its fullness.'

Let us begin – I invite you to picture a place you know well – somewhere special to you – perhaps by the sea, or in a park; perhaps a favourite spot at home or in a garden. Just spend a couple of minutes allowing that picture to emerge for you – remember you do not need to strive or struggle – a picture may come easily to mind or you may just have an inner awareness that connects you with a special place, without being able to see it in detail.

So . . . you are in a place you know well – it is peaceful and calm and you feel relaxed . . . as you look around you, you notice another person sitting nearby, with his head turned slightly away from you so you cannot see who he is. You didn't notice the person before, but now you do – as you look at him, he slowly turns his head – there is a moment of surprise and recognition as you realize that it is Jesus who is sitting there. Let yourself picture that moment of encounter – become aware of how you are feeling and what you are thinking as Jesus looks at you and smiles a gentle smile.

Jesus says: 'I have come that you, ... (hear your own name) might have life – life in all its fullness.'

(The leader gives an example using the names of two of the participants.)

Let the interaction between you and Jesus unfold as you respond to his promise. Stay with the scene as long as you like, until it comes to a natural conclusion . When you are ready, move into the rest of the afternoon – there are more reflection sheets for you to use if you wish.

Choose life! – reflection sheet 2

A meditation on Psalm 81

A visit to the dentist – a routine we all endure
with mouth forced open wide against clenched jaw!

But as I struggled with the tension
of prodding, poking, pulling,
an image came to mind:
a nest of baby birds
mouths wide, open-stretched,
bright-splashed yellow signal
clamouring for food.

And it seemed through them God called to me:
'Choose Life!
Offer yourself completely to all
I desire to give you;
take hold of life afresh with passion and with purpose,
casting off everything that would
hold you back,
turn your head,
pollute your thinking,
sidetrack your journey,
divert your attention
from my Love which is ALL in ALL.'

I came away with clean teeth and a cleansed mind,
encouraged by my God
who chose to meet me even as the dentist drilled.

'Open your mouth wide and I will fill it . . .
I would feed you with the finest of the wheat,
and with honey from the rock
I would satisfy you.'
Psalm 81.10, 16

Choose life! – reflection sheet 3

What is getting in the way of your living life in all its fullness?

You might consider things like your fears,
co-dependent relationships,
issues related to your childhood,
problems with trust,
unhelpful images of God,
addictions and attachments which keep you
from living freely.

Talk to God or Jesus about these things
if it helps you could draw them – stick figures are fine –
or make a diagram or write a list

When you are ready, ask God or Jesus to give you the grace
to begin to leave these things behind
so that you can start to live more abundantly in Christ.

Go for a walk and look for signs of abundant life
around you. Talk to God about what you see.
As you meditate on your discoveries, take time to be still
enough to hear God's gentle voice speaking to you through
the everyday environment.

Stepping out of the boat
Opening worship

SENTENCE OF THE DAY

Peter answered him, 'Lord, if it is you, command me to come to you on the water.'
He said, 'Come.' So Peter got out of the boat, started walking on the water, and
came towards Jesus.
Matthew 14.28–9

Leader   We thank you Lord for bringing us here today, for gathering us together so that we may spend time with you and learn more about your will for us, both as individuals and as a faith community.

All   **Help us Lord to hold fast to you and to our faith; help us to hold lightly those structures which have sustained us in the past, trusting that you will help us to discern a way forward for the future.**

FIRST CANDLE IS LIT

Leader   Often before a new way forward can become a reality there will be a period of exploration, a time of gathering information, of brainstorming possibilities and thinking 'outside the square'.

All   **Help us to be patient with each other's ideas, ready to find the mystery of your invitation in unlikely places. May we dream together and be open to the unexpected movement of grace among us.**

SECOND CANDLE IS LIT

Leader   As we consider new ways of being your people in this place, help us to listen to you and to each other, help us to take each step slowly, in time with your leading, O Holy Spirit of God.

All   **Help us today Lord to learn from you. Direct our thinking so that we may begin to come to a clearer understanding of what you are calling us to be and to do for you in this parish and through our presence in the wider community. Amen.**

THIRD CANDLE IS LIT

Stepping out of the boat – short talk 1

(This Quiet Day provides an opportunity for a parish or group to dream together about the future. It is appropriate when facing change or when wanting to discern a new way of connecting with local community. You may want to begin with a brief acknowledgement of the particular challenges or opportunities which this group faces. For example, a vestry/parish council may be considering different leadership models, OR you may be wondering how to reach out to those in the neighbourhood, to immigrants or young families . . . choose whichever portions of the following material suit your situation. You'll see that I have included several websites and it would be really helpful to have looked at these before facilitating this Quiet Day.)

We cannot deny that the Church as we have known it for decades is facing some challenges – fewer people seem to attend church regularly, there are increasing financial, maintenance and staffing needs, life is full, and people are busy.

But with challenges come opportunities. There is a growing awareness of and interest in spiritual realities among the general population. Building on the work of Alister Hardy,[42] research by David Hay[43] suggests that over 70 per cent of the general population have some sort of spiritual experience, whether or not they would recognize or interpret that experience as somehow being connected with God. Hay comments:

> God the Holy Spirit communicates with all of Creation. From this perspective one might see the mission of the Church as to be alert to – and be in tune with – the ways in which God is already in touch with everybody, inside or outside the Church.[44]

There is a huge potential for new ways of connecting with people and shaping church life afresh – examples of innovative services and programmes offered by churches are beginning to emerge. 'New Way of Being Church' has been active for over a decade in this field and some of their ideas can be seen on their website: www.newway.org.uk. 'Fresh Expressions' www.freshexpressions.org.uk has been set up more recently with the encouragement of the Archbishop of Canterbury and Methodist leaders and already has interesting examples of local projects.

---

42 Hardy, a biologist, founded a centre for the study of religious experience in the 1950s. Originally based at Oxford, the Alister Hardy Research Centre, as it is now known, has relocated to the University of Lampeter in Wales. For more details see their website: www.alisterhardytrust.org.uk

43 See for example David Hay, *Religious Experience Today*, Mowbray, London, 1990.

44 David Hay, *The Spirituality of the Unchurched*, from page 2 of a paper presented at the 2000 Conference of the British and Irish Association for Mission Studies. Full text available on www.martynmission.cam.ac.uk/BIAMSHay.htm

Through such initiatives we are encouraged to honour the best of our tradition while being open to the possibility of God doing a new work in and through us. Those proposing and offering new expressions of church believe that the Holy Spirit can and does engage with willing people to guide us into creative responses which are appropriate for local needs. God through the work of the Holy Spirit helps us reach out to our communities in ways that make sense to contemporary minds and lifestyles, and enables us to address practical and logistical issues related to staffing and finances.

If we take time to listen to God and time to discern what we are hearing, both as individuals and as a group, gradually ways forward will emerge which not only will strengthen our community of faith, but will help meet the needs of our friends and neighbours, and contribute to the country's greater good. We can trust that God can make a perfect match between a community need and the parish's capacity to meet or help meet that need. We can trust that God has within this community of faith both a mission and the skills to fulfil that mission.

We may already be offering support in the neighbourhood; we may feel as though we are doing all that can be done and making the most of available people and resources. However, things don't stand still; situations change. God the Creator encourages us to meet change unafraid, confident that God can and will enable us, not only to find a novel solution to whatever problem we face, but also to determine creative ways of bringing something of the Good News of Jesus Christ into the lives of those around us.

We are encouraged to trust that God can overcome any obstacles if we are honest with God and with each other. It can be challenging to have to set aside our own agendas in order to support a new vision; it can be hard to relinquish power and control so that a new programme can be resourced or a hard choice made. Perhaps something has to come to a natural conclusion before resources can be released to support a new endeavour. There is inevitable pain for those who leave the familiar behind. But – if we listen to God, if we listen to each other in love, just imagine what God might do . . .

The First Reflection sheet invites you to consider how you might feel and what you might think about 'stepping out of the boat' – risking a new level of trust in God.

Stepping out of the boat – reflection sheet 1

Read the story of Peter and, in your imagination,
put yourself in his shoes:
let Jesus invite you
to 'step out of the boat'.

Matthew 14.24–33

PERSONAL

As you reflect on the above passage, let the Holy Spirit bring to your mind the things that you are hanging on to that stop you from stepping out in faith: for example, fears of some sort, or reluctance to deal with change, or wanting to remain comfortable . . .

Consider which aspects of your ministry in this place you would gladly relinquish and which you still feel energy for.
Talk to God about what you have discovered.

PARISH

When you think about your parish, what may need to be set aside to make room for new ways of being church in this community?

What obstacles might hinder exploring new ways forward? Consider, for example, ministry structures / administration / forms of services / mission focus for your parish.

You may like to talk to God about your ideas.

NOTE: There will be time for sharing something of your thinking in the group reflection time later in the day, if you want to do that.

Stepping out of the boat – short talk 2

When we begin to think about new activities or programmes or a rearrangement of resources or personnel, comments like these may surface:

'Well we've tried that before. It didn't work then so why should it work now?'

'I've taken Sunday School for twenty years and there's no one else to take over so what will happen to the children if I stop doing it every week?'

'I am absolutely overstretched now and I can't commit to another weekly service.'

(Add any others which seem to fit your situation.)

Three things stand out as we face such questions.

First, if we have been waiting upon God in prayer, listening for guidance – for example through Scripture, circumstances, prophetic words or pictures, an inner conviction of the Holy Spirit and the wisdom of other mature Christians – we can be confident that we will not be led 'up the garden path'. God will instead lead us into something that is practical, realistic and helpful for those we seek to serve, economical in terms of time and resources, creative and, surprisingly, even *fun*!

We may be led to meet a very simple need such as offering an occasional cake and coffee meeting for new residents or hearing a child's reading in the local primary school or taking an elderly person to a doctor's appointment; it may be something more organized such as providing a weekly homework club or setting up a food-bank; it may be something even bigger such as a call to fight the closure of a health or postal service.

But whatever way forward we discern and no matter how many people 'turn up', instead of our ministry being a struggle or a chore, we will know that this is God's call for our community; we shall be doing this work in God's strength, not our own, and we and others will be blessed.

Second, we find ourselves in a vastly different situation at the start of the twenty-first century from that which we knew even twenty years ago. This is a new time, with different circumstances and a different group of people; with a greater diversity of skills and experience among members of our community, old and young. Although those of us on the far side of fifty may still be trying to get our heads around rapid technological change and a mushrooming of communication opportunities, if we are prepared to include young people in our planning and brainstorming and if we are flexible and open to new possibilities, the Holy Spirit is able to work among us with greater creativity and freedom.

Third, none of us has all the answers. We need each other; honest, caring, respectful communication is essential if we are to dream together and risk offering ideas for discussion. May we hold each other in love as we seek God's vision for this community.

(Invite participants to spend time in personal reflection using Reflection Sheet 2 before gathering them into small groups to consider the following questions. Further questions can be added to suit local circumstances. Groups no bigger than 4 ensure that everyone has a chance to be heard. For each small group have a copy of the questions and ask someone to act as recorder to write down the answers so that some notes of people's ideas can be made available for later discussion where appropriate.)

Small-group discussion questions

1 What would our dream for this parish be?
2 As we think of how we might be God's hands, voice and love among friends and neighbours, what gives us the most energy and joy?
3 What do we sense God may be asking us to consider as a way of engaging afresh with our community? of meeting a need? of offering a service?
4 What do we sense God may be asking us to set aside?

(Once everyone has had time to discuss the questions, gather the group and listen together to the summaries WITHOUT DEBATE OR DISCUSSION.

At the closing, offer these notes as a gift to God and pray for further discernment. You may want to set a time to gather again if something has captured people's hearts and minds.)

Stepping out of the boat – reflection sheet 2

What does God want to bring to birth in you, in the parish or in your neighbourhood?

Read the story of the angel's visit to Mary and her response.
In your imagination, allow yourself to consider what God may want to bring to birth in you and your reaction to God's invitation to be part of God's creative work in the world.

You may like to talk to God about these things and ask for the grace you need to help you say, with Mary,
'Here I am, the servant of the Lord; let it be to me according to your word.'

Luke 1.26–38

Personal	Parish
What is my passion? What do I have energy for? How might that passion or energy find expression in my own life? How might that passion or energy help address a need in the community?	If your parish is facing a time of uncertainty or transition, trust that God has something in mind for this faith community – spend some time listening for ideas and glimpses of what God desires to bring to life in your parish . . .
Name before God any new area of ministry which is beginning to emerge for you and ask for the grace you need to discern the next step.	Although it is early in the discernment process, let yourself dream about how this might take place . . . and be ready to share some of your thoughts in the small-group reflection.

The waiting place of God
Opening worship

SENTENCE OF THE DAY

Those who wait for the LORD *shall renew their strength; they shall mount up with wings like eagles; they shall run, and not be weary; and they shall walk, and not faint.*
Isaiah 40.31

Leader We thank you Lord for bringing us here today, for gathering us together at this point in our own individual journeys, so that we may spend time with you in corporate solitude.

All **Winter is a time of letting go, of entering a silent space, of waiting and trusting that in the course of time, new life will emerge from the darkness. Help us Lord to be mindful of those things that we need to relinquish so that you can bring new life to birth in us. Help us to trust you so that we can welcome the waiting as a time of preparation and quietly creative rest.**

FIRST CANDLE IS LIT

Leader Often before the new can become a reality there will be a period of waiting, yet our society devalues waiting – we're constantly encouraged to look for the quick answer, the shortcut and the simplistic . . . sometimes we think of God in the same way and expect quick answers and a clear way forward when God desires to gift us with the sacrament of waiting.

All **You teach us Lord that we need to wait in order to learn from you; you remind us that your timing is not necessarily the same as ours.**
Help us Lord to receive the waiting with grace, help us to recognize the signs of your presence in the midst of the unknowing – for those reminders will be there if we are still enough to see them.

SECOND CANDLE IS LIT

Leader Some times of waiting are distressing; and we want them to be over with as quickly as possible; other times of waiting are filled with eager anticipation and we let those times go almost with wistfulness. Whether hard or welcomed waiting can be a time of wondering, of striving, of plans made and unmade, of fears and of fancies as our minds try to fill the gap and force the pace of change.

All **Help us Lord to know that you are in the midst of our waiting, whatever the circumstances. May we become aware of the gifts which lie ready to be discovered within the waiting place of God. Amen.**

THIRD CANDLE IS LIT

© Sue Pickering 2006

The waiting place of God – short talk 1

You'll probably remember the TV Programme *Waiting for God* – stories set in a retirement village, and the title implying that people were filling in time until they died. The sort of waiting I had in mind when thinking of a theme for today's Quiet Day was not a 'filling in of time until we die' sort of waiting – but a different sort of waiting – a time between letting go and embracing: the letting go of old patterns, of familiar and comfortable ways of relating to God and people, and the embracing of new challenges, and new ways of understanding ourselves in relation to God.

Waiting is a recurring theme in the Scriptures. For example

- centuries of waiting for the birth of the Messiah foretold by Old Testament prophets
- years spent by Jesus as a carpenter before his public ministry
- days spent by the disciples after the Ascension waiting for the Holy Spirit.

(You can add further examples if you want to, and then spend a little time in pairs or small-group discussion, exploring the way 'waiting' is handled by the biblical characters, before going on.)

Waiting times are not always easy – we may stumble and wander, unsure of the next step – there may even be a sense in which we find it hard to understand where God may be – our prayers may hit the ceiling; we may not be hearing God in the way we have heard God before . . . Or we may have a clear sense of a way forward but circumstances seem to conspire to block our way and hold up our progress – we are impatient and cannot see the reasons for delays and setbacks.

This type of waiting can be a sort of wilderness experience – we can feel isolated and uncertain as our comfortable and familiar signposts disappear . . . but we know from experience that fretting about past events, or being anxious about future possibilities, gets us nowhere and undermines our spiritual well-being.

But things are different if we hold a more positive attitude towards waiting. The contemporary Catholic writer Macrina Wiederkehr speaks of the 'sacrament of waiting'[45] reminding us of the hidden treasure available to us if we simply attend to whatever we find ourselves doing, thinking or facing. If we *are present to the moment*, rather than wondering about the past or trying to second-guess the future, our times of waiting can be enriched. For, if we can but recognize it, during this waiting time, we remain enfolded in the loving purposes of God.

---

45 Macrina Wiederkehr, *Seasons of Your Heart*, HarperSanFrancisco, 1991, p. 7

The waiting place of God – reflection sheet 1

Hear, O LORD, when I cry aloud,
be gracious to me and answer me!
'Come,' my heart says, 'seek his face!'
Your face, LORD, do I seek.
Do not hide your face from me.
Do not turn your servant away in anger,
you who have been my help.
Do not cast me off, do not forsake me,
O God of my salvation!
If my father and mother forsake me,
the LORD will take me up.
Teach me your way, O LORD,
and lead me on a level path . . .

I believe that I shall see the goodness of
the LORD in the land of the living.
Wait for the LORD;
be strong and let you heart take courage;
wait for the LORD!
Psalm 27.7–11, 13–14

On our spiritual journeys,
there are times
when God can seem far away.

If God seems far away from you now,
remember that God is
more faithful than any parent;
have the courage to pray
for the grace you need
to 'reopen' communication.

Find a quiet place out of doors or
somewhere you won't be disturbed.
Sit and notice what is around you.
Let your focus settle on one thing
and let God speak to you
as you wait
and wonder . . .

Where are you at present?

What are you being invited to set aside?

What are you being encouraged to
embrace?

Or are you wandering in circles?

What do you need from God to help you
at this time?

Those who wait for the LORD shall
renew their strength;

they shall mount up with wings like
eagles;

they shall run, and not be weary,
they shall walk, and not faint.
Isaiah 40.31

The waiting place of God – short talk 2

Whether we are in the waiting place of God ourselves at this particular moment or whether we are keeping someone else company during their waiting time, we know that there are some periods of waiting that are harder than others.

We don't find it hard to wait for something hopeful and exciting like the birth of a baby or moving to a new home, and although we might say, 'I just can't wait until . . .' we generally manage the waiting time well.

But there are waiting times that are hard:

- waiting as the date approaches for us to leave our job, through retirement or redundancy
- waiting for the results of medical tests which will determine the shape or even the length of our lives
- waiting, powerless, as a loved one goes through a terminal illness.

Let's think for a moment about Mary, the mother of Jesus, and the different times of waiting she experienced:

- staying with Elizabeth for the first three months of her pregnancy
- then waiting for the birth of Jesus and the journey to Bethlehem as his birth was imminent
- the time of waiting in Egypt until it was safe to return
- the time of waiting to find Jesus in the temple when he was 12
- the time of waiting to know whether or not he would receive the penalty of crucifixion
- the time of waiting at the foot of the cross
- the time of waiting to see his resurrected form appearing to her after Easter morning.

How can we see God's hand in these times of struggle?

Where are the gifts in the waiting?

We have the promise of Scripture that God does not leave us comfortless, that they who wait upon the Lord will renew their strength, that God is faithful and will not leave us or forsake us, and so I invite you to participate in a guided meditation focusing on the gift or gifts which the Holy Spirit may want to reveal to you today, either to reinforce something you are already aware of, or to provide you with a new perspective on a situation which you are currently facing . . .

The waiting place of God – a guided meditation

As always with a guided meditation, it is your choice whether you take part or not. You may prefer simply to listen without thinking about images or trying to make something significant surface. Just trust the Holy Spirit to begin what is right for you at this time – even if you do not become aware of any outcome for some time.

Once I have stopped speaking, either stay with what might have arisen for you or let it go gently. When you are ready you may like to write about or draw something of your experience, or you may prefer to use another way of being attentive to God for the rest of the time we have together.

So let us begin with a prayer:

Loving God, we bring to you this time of reflection using our imaginations.
May your Holy Spirit guide us and protect us, and reveal more of your nature which is Love. Amen.

Make sure that you are comfortable and warm – take a few moments to relax yourself physically. You are invited to close your eyes to minimize distractions. Take a few easy, slow breaths . . . and begin to let yourself settle into the warmth of God.

Take a few moments to recall an area of your life in which you are waiting at present:

- it could be related to matters of lifestyle, a place to live
- a task to take up
- it might be about issues of decision, discernment and choice
- perhaps it is to do with a difficult letting go
- or an anxious time before test results return
- or the joyful anticipation of a homecoming.

Let one particular time of waiting emerge for you.

(Give a minute or two to let this come to mind but not too long or people's analytical mode might begin to interfere!)

Whatever the nature of the waiting is, know that God understands your situation and longs to be there with you in the midst of it all . . .

One way that God can be with you is to provide you with a waiting place – a very special space of your own, where the waiting can unfold. Let your imagination create just such a place for you now.

Don't struggle – just let a detail or two emerge – gradually you will come to some awareness of what this waiting place is like:

- This place might be a room – perhaps there is something on the walls or floor that attracts your attention – or there may be an item of furniture which you notice – look closely at the colours, become aware of any fragrance, any sound or sight that calls you.
- The waiting place may not be a room, it may not even be indoors.
- Perhaps your waiting place is a platform at a station or a cosy nest up in a tree, or a favourite fishing spot. Whatever it is, let your imagination bring it to life for you.

(Provide a good chunk of silence – to let the awareness have time to form either with a visual image or an impression that is not visual but will nevertheless be helpful.)

Now you become aware that God wants to give you a gift –
a unique gift just for you as you wait,
a gift offered with love from the Creator of all.
Let this gift of God gently take form or awareness for you –

Remember that this 'gift' may or may not be something tangible – it could be a quality or attitude rather than something material. If you don't have an awareness of any particular 'gift', talk to God about what you need for your life at this time, especially if you are facing a difficult period of waiting.

(Again provide a chunk of time as above.)

Bring your questions, your thoughts and feelings to God.

Spend as long as you want to in the waiting place of God, before leaving, knowing that God will go with you wherever you go and will wait with you for as long as it takes.

The waiting place of God –reflection sheet 2

If you can, go outside and find an autumn leaf.
Take it and sit with it for ten to fifteen minutes
and let God speak to you through it.

or

write or draw in your journal something about
your experience during the guided meditation

or

use one of the following as an aid to meditation

Read the story of the disciples on the
road to Emmaus.
Luke 24.13–31

Have you felt like them at times – lost,
puzzled, sad, not daring to hope for the
miracle of the new life that God wants
to offer you?

Put yourself in their place and then
reflect on why Jesus waited before he
revealed himself to them.

What was the gift they received
in the waiting?

WAITING

In the darkness the candle waits
for heart and will
and hand and flame
to love, to touch,
to light, to move
passivity into action,
readiness into fulfilment,
potential into reality,
impulse into sight.

In life's darkness my spirit waits
for your warm touch
to heal my shame,
to woo, to win,
to bring me life,
dissolving all my resistance,
opening me to new ways of grace
helping me to enjoy your Love,
and celebrate new life.

Mosaics of mercy
Opening worship

SENTENCE OF THE DAY
Grace and truth came through Jesus Christ.
John 1.17

Leader We come as we are, Loving God, just as we are.

All **We bring with us all the pieces of our lives,**
things that occupy our minds and take our energy:
hopes and fears, tasks and tears,
the trivial and the overwhelming
details of each day.

FIRST CANDLE IS LIT

Leader Help us to approach this time
with confidence,
knowing that you always want
what is best for us and those we love.

All **Help us to become aware**
of the ways you have
met us and supported us,
down through the years,
shaping a mosaic of mercy
in our lives.

SECOND CANDLE IS LIT

Leader May we be given a glimpse
of the riches of your grace,
made accessible through the One
in whom your Love took flesh and form.

All **May your Holy Spirit**
reveal to us the depth and breadth
of your Love for us
and the ways in which we can be
bearers of that Love to others.
Amen.

THIRD CANDLE IS LIT

Mosaics of mercy – short talk 1

Making sense of our experience, those things which draw or drive us, can be hard. Our lives can seem like bits of broken pottery or coloured tiles – but reflection and focus can transform them into something beautiful for God.

Many of us have seen mosaics in churches, or perhaps in the ruins of Roman villas – we may be aware of contemporary mosaics in gardens or galleries. We are conscious of the hundreds, perhaps thousands of pieces of tiles or stones which have been painstakingly crafted together over a long period of time.

(If you are fortunate enough to be meeting in a place where there are stained-glass windows, you can point out particular features before continuing.)

A stained-glass window, for example, is a type of mosaic. Each piece on its own may seem insignificant, limited in beauty or usefulness, but together these pieces make up a unique expression of worship, crafted by people bearing God's image.

On our faith journeys God has been present to us in all sorts of ways.

(If you wish, ask participants to share briefly how they have been aware of God in their lives, some of the things, events and so forth, which have shaped their spiritual journeys so far . . . or give a few minutes' silence for reflection.)

Some of the things that you may have thought about include:

- particular Scripture passages which have been pivotal
- dreams
- people who have helped us
- special places where we have felt close to God
- times of great trial when we have known ourselves held in love
- surprises
- hymns, songs and other music which has nourished us
- symbols which God has used to help us deepen our awareness.

God has over the years come to us in all sorts of different ways, not just through creation or Scripture or the expected vehicles of our tradition, liturgy and corporate worship. So, Reflection Sheet 1 this morning will offer you a chance to reflect on the way God's presence/leading/influence has been apparent in your life's mosaic.

But – our lives are not lived in isolation. We are made for community.

Each one of us plays a part in the collage of compassion which God is creating in other people's lives, and Reflection Sheet 2 this morning helps you consider how your life intersects with the lives of others around you – in the past and in the present.

If you are in a state of transition or are feeling disconnected, you may want to talk to God about what you would hope for in terms of being there for other people . . . it may be that you are at a stage in your life when you are living alone or less able to get out and about – if so, God will still give you ways of connecting with others, in prayer and in small practical expressions of care.

Life is so full that many of us rarely stop, but today there is time for us to recall some of the ways in which God has been creating a mosaic of mercy, a collage of compassion with and through us as we have journeyed through life.

A *word or two about collage:*

There are several ways of doing this:

- cutting out pictures and assembling/arranging them
- cutting out small pieces of coloured paper and shaping these pieces into patterns and pictures
- using letters and shapes to express something of what is going on for you and God
- combining cut-out pictures with your own drawing /writing
- using different sizes of paper: A4 or A3
- using glue sticks or magic dots to stick things on!!

To move us into a contemplative space – consider the Tabgha mosaic as we listen to some quiet music. When you are ready, move off into your own reflection time.

You may like to spend some time colouring in this mosaic, modelled on the ancient mosaic found at Tabgha on the banks of the Sea of Galilee, and recalling the miracle of the Loaves and Fishes . . .

Mosaics of mercy – reflection sheet 1

'How has God been forming a mosaic of mercy in my life over the years?'

There are two possible activities. Rather than trying to do both, begin by resting in God, and letting God give you the starting point.

Read Mark 6.35–44. Spend some time looking at the Tabgha mosaic which depicts the miracle of the feeding of the five thousand when little pieces of bread and fish were fashioned into a miraculous meal for thousands – a reminder that nothing is impossible with God. When you are ready, ask God to help you 'colour in the pieces' very slowly – perhaps letting each piece represent one of your experiences of God, or a glimpse of mercy or grace in your life. As you shade or colour in the tiles, you may like to talk to God, sharing your heart's desires or you may just like to be quiet, letting your spirit be open to the tender touch of God.	Let God speak to you as you make a collage – you may like to consider and include some of the following: • the influences that have shaped you • the people who have supported you or helped you grow in God • glimpses of God's grace, for example in creation • key Scripture passages • dreams • special places where you have felt close to God • times of great trial when you have known yourself held in love • surprises • music which has nourished you • symbols which God has used to connect with you.

When you have finished your colouring or collage or other prayer, reflect on the process:

• What was it like doing this?
• What did I discover about my life's journey so far?
• What did I discover about myself? about God?
• What might I take from this exercise into my spiritual life?

Mosaics of mercy – reflection sheet 2

'How is God including me in the mosaics of mercy he is shaping in the lives of those around me?'

'You shall love the Lord your God with all your heart, and with all your soul, and with all your strength, and with all your mind; and your neighbour as yourself.'
Luke 10.27

Sit with God and reflect on those people/places/groups with whom you have a connection.

They may be family, friends, members of a group you attend, old neighbours or workmates.

You may want to make a 'collage of compassion' to express something about what you bring to these relationships.

Or you may want to make a diagram or draw or write something to help you uncover the pattern of those connections and how God may be touching people through you.

Sit with God and consider one person for whom you feel really heavily responsible – to the point of it being a burden or a challenge.

Take a clean sheet of paper and put that person on the page in some way – then put yourself on the page. Let God bring to mind other things/people/events which may be helping or supporting that person.

If you are not aware of any such things/people/events, then put God's love on the page in some way and offer yourself and this person to God.

You may like to pray that God's grace will flow into this person's life in a new way and that your sense of burden may be relieved by the Burden-bearer, our Lord Jesus Christ.

For whom are you Christ's hands or voice ?
What do you need from God to help you as you re-present Christ in your community?

Mosaics of mercy – short talk 2

(Begin with a short time of discussion based on the following.)

As you have spent time reflecting on the way that God has been building a mosaic of mercy in your life – what have you noticed?

- perhaps that there were a number of different people who have been influential, or helpful or challenging
- perhaps that God has connected with you in surprising ways
- that different things/people have been significant at different times in your spiritual life.

What about the way God has placed you, or is placing you, in other people's lives?

- Are you the only practising Christian in your family?
- Perhaps you have had a surprise encounter with someone lately?
- Do you find yourself being a 'listening ear' to others with problems?

(Then move into the following input designed to encourage a practice of regular reflection at the day's end.)

I mentioned earlier how hard it can be for us to see patterns and themes if we do not spend time regularly waiting on God in openness. One way of helping us develop such a practice is the old spiritual discipline of the *examen* – a daily opportunity for reflection on both the unhelpful and the helpful aspects of our personalities, inter-actions, experiences of God and other people.

To illustrate the value of this practice, the Linns, in their book *Sleeping with Bread: Holding what Gives You Life,* share a story from the Second World War:

> During the bombing raids of WWII, thousands of children were orphaned and left to starve. The fortunate ones were rescued and placed in refugee camps where they received food and good care. But many of these children could not sleep at night, fearing waking up to find themselves once again homeless and without food. Finally someone hit upon the idea of giving each child a piece of bread to hold at bedtime. Holding their bread, these children could finally sleep in peace. All through the night the bread reminded them, 'Today I ate and I will eat again tomorrow.'[46]

---

46 Dennis Linn, Sheila Fabricant Linn and Matthew Linn, *Sleeping with Bread: Holding what Gives You Life,* Paulist Press, New York, 1995, p. 1.

Each day we ask for, and are given, bread by God. As with our normal food, all too often we eat this 'bread' without really noticing its goodness. The Linns invite us to take the time to 'hold our bread', to look for the challenges and the gifts of each day, as we make a mosaic of mercy from the pieces of our lives.

In its simplest form, the examen can mean asking ourselves pairs of questions to help us identify the 'consolations' and 'desolations' in our lives – 'the interior movements through which divine revelation unfolds'.[47] Such questions might include: 'For what am I most grateful today? For what am I least grateful?'[48] Where was I most aware of God today? Where was I least aware of God today? Through this process, we gradually learn to recognize those things which give us life and energy or which drag us down. We begin to identify patterns in our responses which might need our attention, such as a tendency to keep silent instead of speaking out about something important, or to react defensively when someone is trying to give us feedback. We are helped to attend to our feelings, and find our unique way of giving and receiving love, our personal 'sealed orders' from God.

A summary of the examen process as suggested by the Linns follows:

- Set aside ten to twenty minutes. Do whatever helps you to relax. For example, light a candle, play some short reflective music, breathe in the love of God and breathe out your cares.
- Place your hand on your heart and ask Jesus or God or the Holy Spirit to bring to your heart the moment today for which you are most grateful.
- Ask God to bring to your heart the moment today for which you are least grateful. Let your feelings come to the surface. You may wish to take deep breaths and let God's love fill you just the way you are.
- Give thanks for whatever you have experienced. You may like to journal your learnings or share them with a family member or friend.[49]

By adapting the questions to suit different ages, this practice can also be integrated into small-group or family reflection or prayer time, and is accessible even to younger children.

Holding on to the good from each day is especially important when we are struggling or feeling a bit overwhelmed or disconnected from God. The EXAMEN can be daily nourishment from God, which, over time, forms a habit of thanksgiving, gives a glimpse into movements of God's grace, reveals signs of hope in the midst of grief, gives insights into areas of struggle and challenge, allows an awareness of unfolding call, and promotes a deeper appreciation and experience of God and of ourselves, as God's people.

---

47 Ibid., p. 19.
48 Ibid., p. 30.
49 Ibid., p. 30.

Mosaics of mercy – reflection sheet 3

Which pairs of questions will I use to begin this practice? For example,

- What has been most/least life-giving today?
- How have I been most aware of God/least aware of God today?
- When have I felt most fully myself/ least fully myself today?

You may like to use one of the above or write your own.

. . . .
. . . .
. . . .

How might I incorporate this spiritual discipline into my evening routine?

. . . .
. . . .
. . . .

How can I safeguard 10–15 minutes for this sacred time with myself and God?

. . . .
. . . .
. . . .

How might this practice be applied in other contexts, such as with friends or family members, in the midst of a liturgy, in a small group setting?

. . . .
. . . .
. . . .

> The place God calls you to is the place where your deep gladness
> and the world's deep hunger meet.
> *Frederick Buechner*[50]

---

50 Frederick Buechner, *Wishful Thinking: A Theological ABC*, HarperCollins, New York, 1973, p. 95.

Part Three
Prayers and blessings for use in closing worship

Prayers and blessings for use in closing worship

(In some traditions deacons or lay people use 'us' and 'our' instead of 'you' and 'your' when offering a blessing.)

Homecoming

Dear God, you are our home. You call us whenever we wander; you remind us of your limitless love and faithfulness. We thank you for all that we have discovered today; we entrust you with our questions; we invite your Holy Spirit to continue the work begun this day, and to help us come home, again and again, to you. Through Jesus Christ our Lord, Amen.

May the God of welcome
run to meet us
with arms outstretched.
May our Brother Jesus
greet us with a smile.
May the Spirit dance us
into the Kingdom,
home safe at last.
Amen.

Retreat and advance

As we return to homes and the daily busyness, to the noise and demands of contemporary living, help us, O Lord of life, to recognize those times when we need to 'retreat' in order to 'advance'. Help us to claim times of reflection and silence so we may listen for your love and grow in our faith. Help us to keep our eyes on you, the One who is the still point in a whirling world. Amen.

May God, giver of living water
touch our thirsty souls;
May the refreshing life of Jesus
invigorate our being;
May the renewing energy of Spirit
flow brightly through us
into our community of faith, of family, of friends.
Amen.

Crampons and crevasses

Hold us, O Strength of our hearts.
Rescue us, O Saviour and Friend.
Anchor us, O Guiding Spirit
that we may know ourselves kept in the security
that only you can bring, in that peace
which, indeed, passes all understanding. Amen.

> May the blessing of God, the One who calls and
> the One who challenges,
> be with each one of us,
> now and for ever.
> Amen.

Rolling back the stone

O Shaper of stones,
O Builder of faith,
we bring to you this day's discoveries,
we offer you our questions,
we share with you the pain of aching hearts,
we give thanks as we remember those who have helped us come closer to you.
Help us to welcome your invitation to fullness of life;
may we be there for other people, doing our part
to help stones of addiction, disappointment, frailty and loneliness roll away,
so the surprising joy of resurrection may be revealed in their lives.
Through Jesus Christ, the risen One. Amen.

> May God, embracing, holding us all, be with us as we go from this place.
> May we carry into our community, the fragrance and freshness of God's love.
> Amen.

The foolishness of God

O God, you challenge us as we see the need for people
to speak against poverty, to challenge unjust structures,
to work for change.
To those of us who are nervous about being 'a fool for Christ',
give a manageable opportunity and enough courage to begin.
To those of us who are already working for justice,
give wisdom and strength as we seek to bring your Kingdom
into being in . . . (*you may like to name something that is relevant to your group,
such as a drop-in centre, a fair trade shop, a lobby group for immigrants, a
homework programme for disadvantaged children*).
We ask this through Jesus, who lived his life for others,
and died to release your Loving Spirit into the world. Amen.

> May the warmth of God's love surround us;
> May the direct gaze of Jesus penetrate our pride;
> May the movement of the Spirit enlarge our hearts;
> and the Blessing of God,
> Radical Creator,
> Unashamed Redeemer and
> Abundant Life-Giver
> be with us and with all whom we serve, now and always.
> Amen.

Transition

We give thanks O God for your faithfulness.
In all our changes, your love supports us, reminding us that,
in Jesus, we have a God who knows both suffering and resurrection.
When we are in the depths, help us to recognize your light.
When we are on the mountaintops, help us to breathe in your joy.
When we are in a no-man's land of uncertainty,
help us hold on to you in trust.
We ask this through Jesus, who has been this way before. Amen.

> Blessed be God who calls us from comfort to risk
> Blessed be God who stays with us when we are afraid
> Blessed be God who shares our trembling and our transitions,
> our disasters and our discoveries.
> May God be praised and exalted above all, for ever.
> Amen.

What's in a name?

O God of many names, teach us to be alert for new ways of naming your presence in our lives. Help us to let go of old punishing labels, carried for decades in the recesses of our souls. Within those spaces, may the fresh wind of your Spirit sing words of grace, helping us to see and name ourselves as beloved and precious in your sight. Amen.

May God, who gives birth to us in pain and passion, hold us close,
so we may hear our name called with love. And the blessing of God,
World-weaver, Hand-holder, Breath-bringer,
enfold us now and evermore.
Amen.

Greed and grace

You are God, opening arms wide to hold the world.
You are God, sharing the riches of creation with each one of us.
You are God, giving of yourself eternally
and we worship you.
In you there is no greed, only grace
and for this, aware of our poverty of heart,
we give you thanks.
Amen.

or

When we are afraid, help us look to you, O Jesus.
Help us to open our clenched fists;
help us to hold out our hands in readiness
and joyful expectation,
like children at Christmas.
Help us receive
and enjoy
the life-gift which you offer each one of us,
every moment of every day.
Amen.

May the grace of our Lord Jesus Christ, and the love of God and the fellowship of the Holy Spirit, be with us now and evermore. Amen.

Choose life!

O Holy Wisdom of God,
empower our discernment,
that we may make Godly choices,
choices which will heal and not harm,
choices which will draw us closer to you, not drive us further away.
In you, O God, may we find abundant life.
With the Spirit's guidance may we
share the Good News with others.
We ask these things through Jesus Christ,
whose choices bought our freedom.
Amen.

Bless us O God with the fruit of your Spirit:
may love, joy, peace,
patience, kindness, goodness,
gentleness, faithfulness and self-control,
be renewed and deepened in us day by day.
Bless those with whom we live, among whom we move,
that in us they may see something of your light and hope,
and make choices which will bring them
closer to you, one gentle step at a time.
Amen.

Stepping out of the boat

Creator God, we thank you for the chance to consider our parish life and your call
to be the voice and hands of Christ in our community. We offer these notes which
contain something of our thoughts and ideas, and ask that your Holy Spirit guide us
in further discernment as we explore the way in which you would have us live out the
gospel in this place. Thank you for being able to dream together. Amen.

May the Wisdom of God inform our thinking,
May the Love of Jesus warm our hearts,
May the Joy of the Spirit bring lightness to our steps,
May we indeed be Christ-bearers to our world.
So may the blessing of God's Wisdom, Love and Joy be with us
and among us now and always.
Amen.

The waiting place of God

All-knowing God, we bring to you the thoughts and feelings of this day. As the natural world enters a time of waiting until new life emerges in the spring, so may we be reminded of the value hidden within our own times of waiting. Deepen in us such a sense of trust in your timing and provision, that we may wait with grace instead of gritted teeth. Amen.

or

O Holy God, as we navigate the commercial maze which threatens to overwhelm the awe-full mystery of the Christ child's birth, help us keep our focus on the joy and simplicity of your coming to us in a form we can embrace. Amen.

May God weave patience into our hearts and minds, into our souls and bodies as we wait for signs of new life. May God give us the insight to recognize signs of grace, and the audacity to dream with the Spirit.
And the blessing of God, the challenge and cherishing of God, be with us now and always. Amen.

Mosaics of mercy

Creator God,
somehow, from the bits and pieces of our days, you make something of beauty.
You transform the 'ugly stuff' of pain and challenge into a mosaic of mercy, and reveal your Love at work in our lives and in the lives of those around us. Encourage us to be gentle with our own and others' brokenness.
Help us to co-operate with you even when we cannot see the whole picture. Deepen our trust as we begin to develop a habit of thankfulness.
Amen.

Blessed be God who calls us to grow and grapple with change;
Blessed be God who offers us healing, whether through hardship or deep joy,
Blessed be God who makes of our lives a mosaic of mercy, an enduring witness to the power of Love at work in the world.
Amen.

Appendix

Recipe for basic playdough

Ingredients

1 cup flour	½ cup salt
1 tbsp cooking oil	2 tsp cream of tartar
1 cup water	food colouring

Method

Mix all ingredients together in a pot. Cook, stirring until mixture leaves the sides of the pot. Take out and roll into a ball.

(Amanda Norris contributed this recipe to the Lytton Street School *Centennial Cookbook*, Feilding, New Zealand, 2001, p. 104.)

Sample programme handout for a Quiet Day

This programme draws heavily on the National Retreat Association Brochure (UK).

The section on 'Hints for making the most of the silence' can be found
on www.retreats.org.uk/leaflets/leaflt15.htm
This prayer from Mother Teresa is widely available. See for example
www.geocities.com/athens/2960/meetmot.htm

The programme is printed on an A4 sheet of paper (landscape layout) and folded
in half. It is easy to make your own, but if you prefer, a template for the full-size
version is available as a Word document or .rtf file by emailing
suepickering@xtra.co.nz

Making the most of the silence . . . *ideas for people who may not be used to coming on a Quiet Day*	Quiet Day *'theme'* *'date'* *'venue'* Conductor: *'name'*
Welcome to this Quiet Day . . . *insert specific timetable and other details for your group*	*insert a verse from Scripture, a prayer or poem or symbol that links with the theme*

Quiet Day

'[Theme]'

[Date]
[Venue]
Conductor: [Name]

Hints for making the most of the silence

1. Do nothing at all . . . just 'be' . . . sit or kneel or lie down and wait for God to lead, to speak, to put ideas and thoughts and pictures and prayers into the mind. Rest and relax in the Lord.

2. Weather permitting, go and enjoy being outside.

3. Use something to 'spark off' your prayer: meditate on a Bible passage related to the theme, or use some of the material provided; pray the words of a favourite hymn or song or use a prayer from the Prayer Book.

4. Use the time to have an honest talk to God about where you are at . . . face up to yourself and your particular needs, trusting that God will deal with these if you give him time and room.

5. Think about your current prayer life and ask God if he desires to show you any new ways of praying.

6. Spend some time journalling . . . writing and drawing your ideas and explorations about your life and where God seems to be . . . or about his absence . . . then talk to God about what you have written.

7. Use coloured pens and paper to express what is happening for you at this particular time in your life.

8. Feel free to spend time talking with the retreat conductor if an issue arises which you want help to explore.

Welcome to this Quiet Day . . .

may it be a time of blessing for you.

A plan of the day follows . . . you are free to take or leave any part of it depending on your own situation (*times are approximate*).

9.30   Gather for tea/coffee and a chat

10.00   A brief introduction to the concept of the Quiet Day and to Silence

10.15   Opening worship followed by a short talk on the theme

10.30   Silence begins (*see back of sheet for suggestions*)

12.00   Prayer at midday from the NZPB (*optional, in the chapel*)

12.15   Please take your lunch when you are ready. Silence is maintained – quiet music will be playing in our lounge

12.45   A second short talk will be followed by a guided meditation on Scripture (*optional*) and further time for silent reflection

2.00   Gathering in the lounge for the closing Eucharist

2.30   Home-going

The fruit of silence is prayer
The fruit of prayer is faith
The fruit of faith is love
The fruit of love is service
The fruit of service is peace.
Mother Teresa of Calcutta

Bibliography

Bausch, William J., *A World of Stories for Preachers and Teachers*, 23rd Publications, Mystic, Connecticut, 1998.

Bonhoeffer, Dietrich, *The Cost of Discipleship*, Macmillan, New York, 1963.

Coffman, Mary Ruth (ed.), *alive now! SILENCE*, Upper Room, Nashville, Nov./Dec. 1990.

Cowley, Joy, *Aotearoa Psalms: Prayers of a New People*, Pleroma Christian Supplies, New Zealand, 2004.

Fischer, Kathleen, *Autumn Gospel: Women in the Second Half of Life*, Paulist Press, New Jersey, 1995.

Foster, Richard, *Prayer: Finding the Heart's True Home*, Hodder & Stoughton, London, 1992.

Hall, Thelma, *Too Deep for Words*, Paulist Press, New Jersey, 1988.

Halpin, Marlene, *Imagine That! Using Phantasy in Spiritual Direction*, Wm. C. Brown, Iowa, 1982.

Hay, David, *Religious Experience Today*, Mowbray, London, 1990.

Hay, David, *The Spirituality of the Unchurched*, from p. 2 of a paper presented at the Conference of the British and Irish Association for Mission Studies in 2000. See www.martynmission.cam.ac.uk/BIAMSHay.htm for full text.

Haskins, Minnie Louise, *The Desert*, privately printed 1908.

Holmes, T. H. and R. H. Rahe, 'The Social Readjustment Rating Scale', *Journal of Psychosomatic Research* 11, 1967.

Huggett, Joyce, *Open to God*, Hodder & Stoughton, London, 1989.

Keating, Thomas, *Open Heart: the Contemplative Dimension of the Gospel*, Continuum, London, 2002.

Keating, Thomas, *Foundations for Centring Prayer and the Christian Contemplative Life*, Continuum International, New York, 2004.

Kiefer, James E, *Teresa of Avila*, www.justus.anglican.org/resources/bio/268.html

Leech, Kenneth, *We Preach Christ Crucified*, Darton, Longman & Todd, London, 1994.

Linn, Dennis, Sheila Fabricant Linn and Matthew Linn, *Sleeping with Bread: Holding what Gives You Life*, Paulist Press, New York, 1995.

Michael, Chester E. and Marie C. Norrisey, *Prayer and Temperament: Different Prayer Forms for Different Personality Types*, The Open Door, Virginia, 1991.

Muggeridge, Malcolm, *Something Beautiful for God*, Collins, London, 1971.

Nouwen, Henri, *With Open Hands*, Ave Maria, Indiana, 1995.

Palmer, Alister, www.newway.org.uk, *New Way of Being Church*, Wells, Somerset BA5 2PD, Tel: 01749 679933.

Pepper, Margaret (ed.), *The Macmillan Dictionary of Religious Quotations*, Macmillan, London, 1996.

Peterson, Eugene, H., *The Message: The New Testament in Contemporary Language*, NavPress, Colorado, 1993.

Powell, John, *He Touched Me*, Argus, Niles, Illinois, 1974.

Pritchard, Sheila, *The Lost Art of Meditation: Deepening your Prayer Life*, Scripture Union, Bletchley, UK, 2003.

Saward, John, *Perfect Fools: Folly for Christ's Sake in Catholic and Orthodox Spirituality*, Oxford University Press, Oxford, 1991.

Sharp, Julie, *Oliver Cornwell*, Paternoster, 1998.

Thomas à Kempis, *The Imitation of Christ*, trans. E. M. Blaiklock, Hodder & Stoughton, London, 1979.

Whyte, Alexander, *Lord, Teach Us to Pray*, Harper & Brothers, New York (undated).

Wiederkehr, Macrina, *Seasons of Your Heart*, HarperSanFrancisco, 1991.